Colored Pencil Step by Step

With Pat Averill, Sylvester Hickmon, and Debra K. Yaun

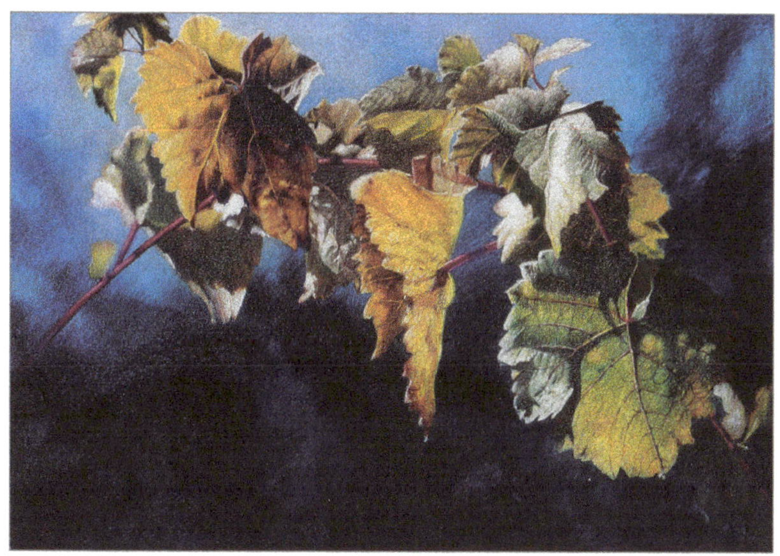

Hope Is Yours for the Seeking by Pat Averill

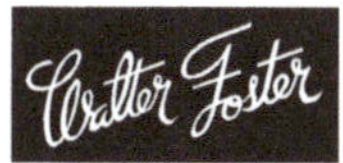

Contents

Quarto.com • WalterFoster.com

First published in 2003 by Walter Foster Publishing, an imprint of The Quarto Group. 100 Cummings Center, Suite 265D, Beverly, MA 01915, USA.
T (978) 282-9590 **F** (978) 283-2742

ISBN: 978-1-56010-719-4

Introduction

Colored pencil is a simple, versatile medium—it can be used to replicate the look of oils, watercolor, acrylic, and more. Although it has been used as a fine art medium for less than a century, its popularity has grown significantly over the last few decades. It's easy to understand why more and more artists are attracted to colored pencils—they are fairly inexpensive and convenient to transport. They are also nontoxic, easy to find in art and craft stores, and combine well with other media. Whether you choose to use colored pencils for sketches or to create fully rendered drawings, you will find that they are brightly hued and precise tools that are a joy to work with.

There are many different approaches and techniques to discover in colored pencil art—from layering and hatching to burnishing and blending. As you explore this art form, you'll discover many methods and materials that will help you realize the seemingly endless creative possibilities working with colored pencil offers. The important thing is to have fun while you develop your own artistic style—and enjoy creating your own works of art in colored pencil!

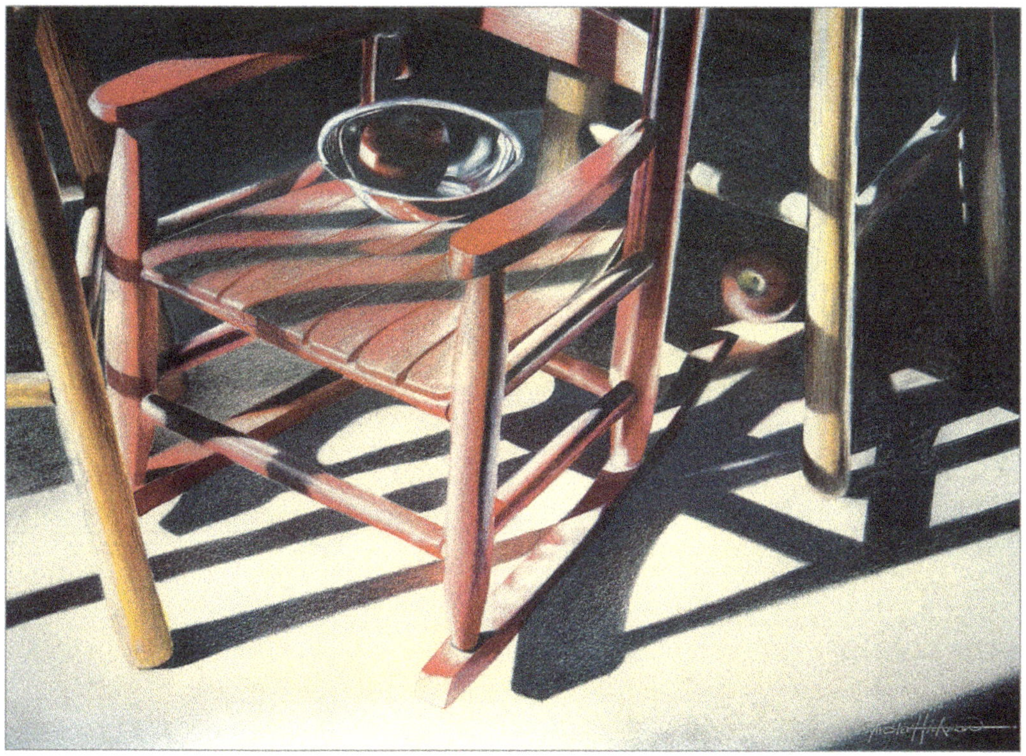

Little Red Rivals by Sylvester Hickmon

Tools and Materials

You don't need many supplies to get started in colored pencil; all you need are a few basic colors, an eraser, a sharpener, and some paper. (See "Color Palettes" on pages 16–17 for the colors the artists use in their lessons). Try to buy the best supplies you can afford; with better-quality supplies, your artwork will stay as vibrant and colorful over time as it did when you first created it. After you've become more familiar with the variety of effects you can create, you may want to purchase a few more specialized tools.

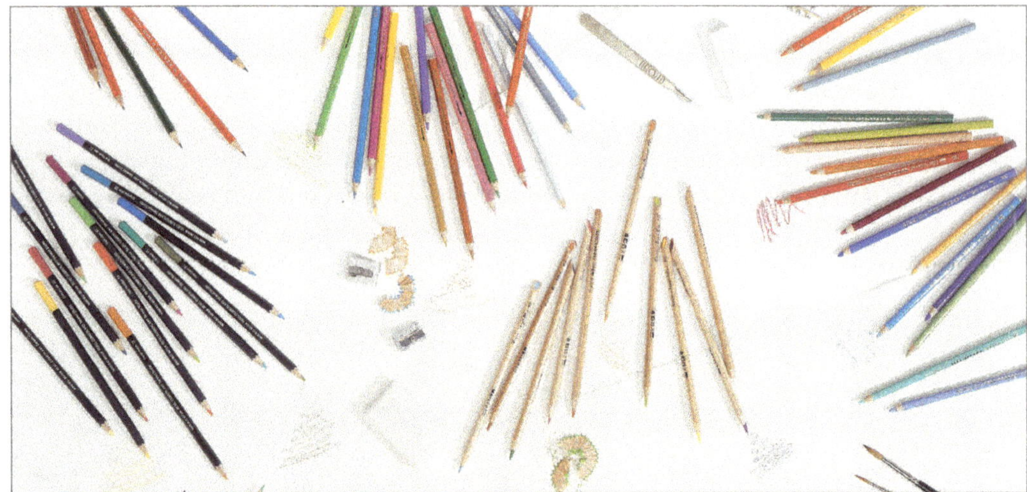

Choosing Pencils There are many types of colored pencils available—harder, thinner leads are ideal for rendering fine lines and detail, whereas softer, thicker leads are great for filling in large areas. Some manufacturers make both hard, thin lead and soft, thick lead versions of the same colors. Experiment to find which types you prefer.

Pencils

As with all art supplies, the price of a pencil indicates its quality; better pencils have truer color. Many brands offer sets of pencils that provide a basic array of colors. Some art stores also sell colored pencils individually—this way you can pick and choose which hues you like best among several different brands. Once you've chosen your palette, make sure to store your pencils upright or safely in a container—and try not to drop them. The lead in a colored pencil is very brittle, and it's likely to break in the shaft if the pencil is dropped. This may not be immediately apparent, but will eventually render the pencil useless.

Erasers

Colored pencil artists can't use ordinary erasers to correct their work; the friction between a rubber or vinyl eraser and the paper will actually melt the wax pigment and flatten the *tooth* (or grain) of the paper. Instead many artists use a small battery-powered eraser to remove the pigment without crushing the paper underneath. A kneaded eraser is also useful for removing small amounts of color; twist or pinch it into any shape you like and then press it lightly on the page to pick up the pigment. When it gets "dirty" and is not as effective, you can knead it (like dough) thoroughly to reveal a clean surface.

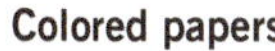

Colored papers

Textured papers

Papers

Textured papers are best for colored pencil work because the rough grain "catches" more pigment than smooth papers do. Art and craft stores carry a variety of textured watercolor papers and illustration boards that offer a good tooth for colored pencil art; look for a paper with a medium grain to start. For practice, you'll want to have a sketch pad or sketchbook. Consider experimenting with different colored papers and specialty papers; these surfaces can help you achieve some interesting effects. (See "Special Papers" on page 13.)

Sharpeners

You can achieve various effects depending on how sharp or dull your pencil is, but generally you'll want to make sure your pencils are sharpened at all times; a sharp point will ultimately provide a smoother layer of color. Although a small hand-held sharpener will do, an electric or battery-operated sharpener is better suited for fine art purposes. You can also use a sandpaper pad to refine a pencil point.

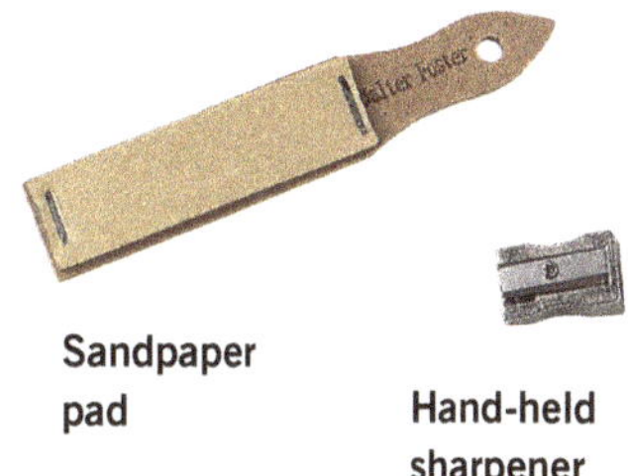

Sandpaper pad

Hand-held sharpener

Extras

You'll need a dust brush to gently remove the pencil residue from your paper, a spray-on fixative to preserve your finished drawing, and a paper blending stump to create soft blends. A pencil extender is handy when the pencil gets too short to hold onto comfortably, and you may want a triangle for making straight lines and some artists' tape for masking. It's also nice to have white gouache and a small brush on hand for adding tiny opaque highlights.

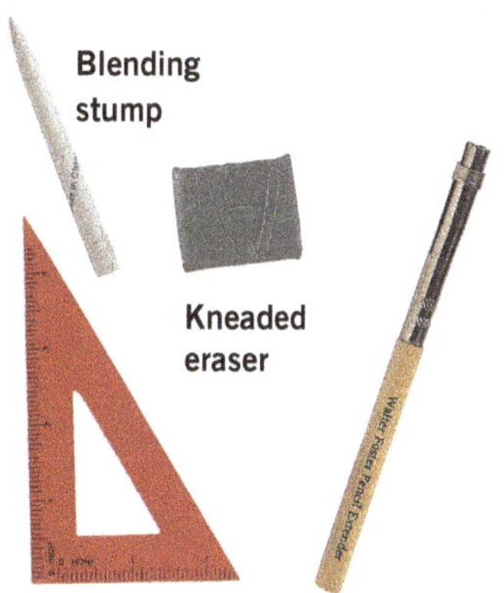

Blending stump

Kneaded eraser

Triangle

Pencil extender

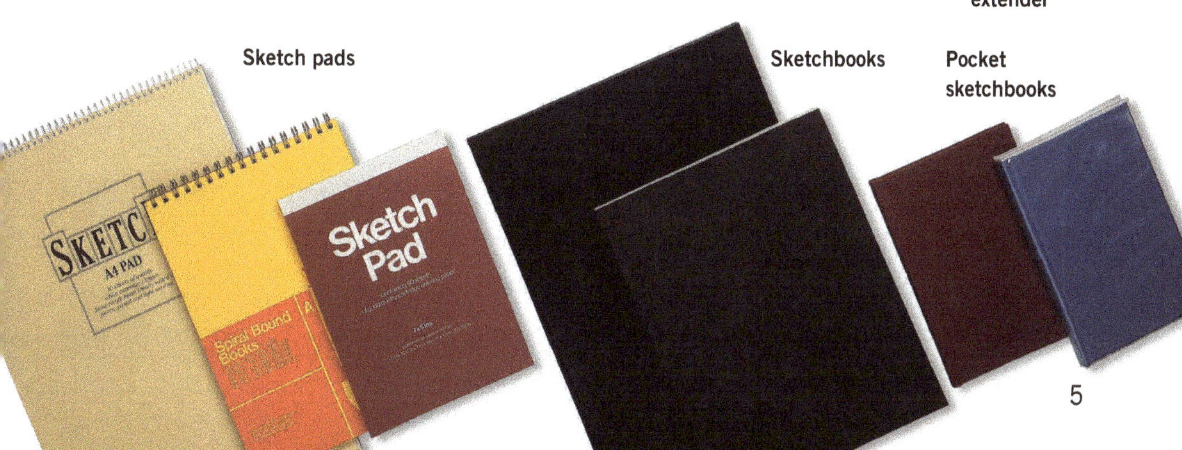

Sketch pads

Sketchbooks

Pocket sketchbooks

Color Theory

Colored pencils are transparent by nature, so instead of "mixing" colors as you would for painting, you create blends by layering colors on top of one another. Knowing a little about basic color theory can help you tremendously in drawing with colored pencils. The *primary* colors (red, yellow, and blue) are the three basic colors that can't be created by mixing other colors; all other colors are derived from these three. *Secondary* colors (orange, green, purple) are each a combination of two primaries, and *tertiary* colors (red-orange, red-purple, yellow-orange, yellow-green, blue-green, blue-purple) are a combination of a primary color and a secondary color. *Hue* refers to the color itself, such as blue or purple, and *intensity* means the strength or *chroma* of a color (usually gauged by pressure applied or pencil quality in colored pencil).

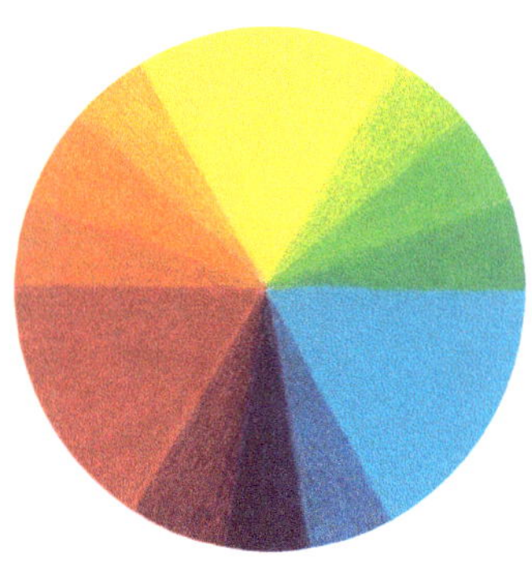

Color Wheel A color wheel can be a useful reference tool for under-standing color relationships. Knowing where each color lies on the color wheel makes it easy to understand how colors relate to and react with one another.

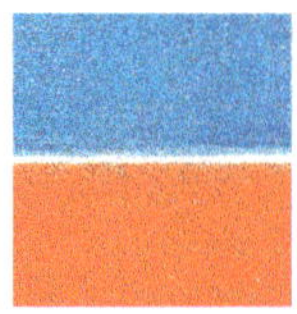

Using Complements When placed next to each other, complementary colors create lively, exciting contrasts. Using a complementary color in the background will cause your subject to seem to "pop" off the canvas.

Complementary Colors

Complementary colors are any two colors directly across from each other on the color wheel (such as red and green, orange and blue, or yellow and purple). You can actually see combinations of complementary colors in nature—for instance, if you look at white clouds in a blue sky, you'll notice a hint of orange in the clouds.

Value

Value is the term used to describe the relative lightness or darkness of a color (or of black). It is the manipulation of values that creates the illusion of form in a drawing, as shown in the sphere on page 7.

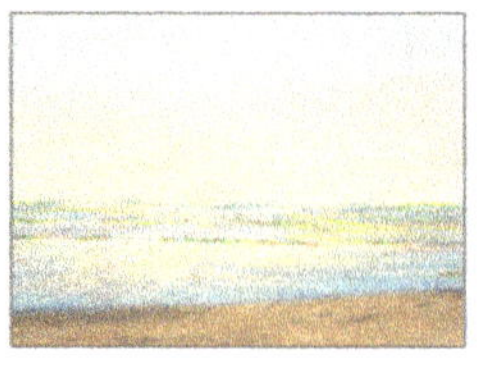
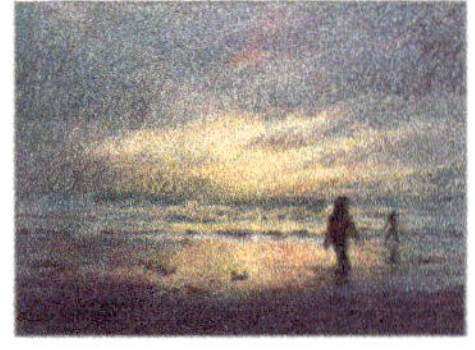

High Key Versus Low Key A high key drawing is filled with light values and evokes an airy, carefree feeling (left), while a low key drawing uses mostly dark values and creates a more mysterious or somber mood (right).

Grays Most colored pencil brands offer a variety of grays. They distinguish them by naming them either "warm" (top row) or "cool" (bottom row) and then adding a percentage to indicate the concentration of color, such as "cool gray 20%" (the lower the percentage, the lighter the value).

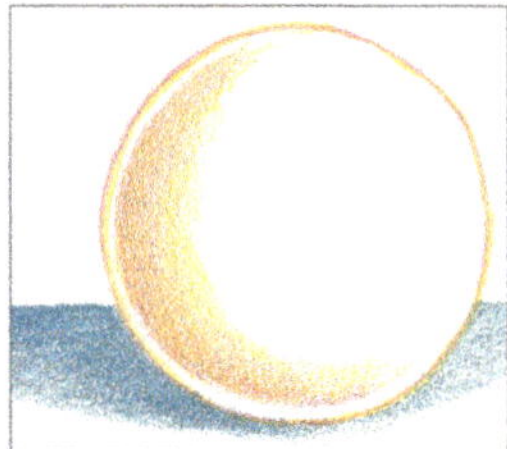

Creating Form Draw the basic shape. Then, starting on the shadowed side, begin building up color, leaving the paper white in the area where the light hits directly.

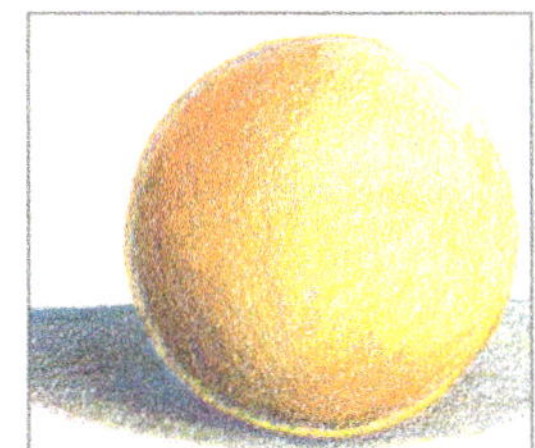

Varying Values Continue adding color, gradually deepening the values to create the spherical form of the ball. Squint your eyes to blur the details, so you can focus on the value changes.

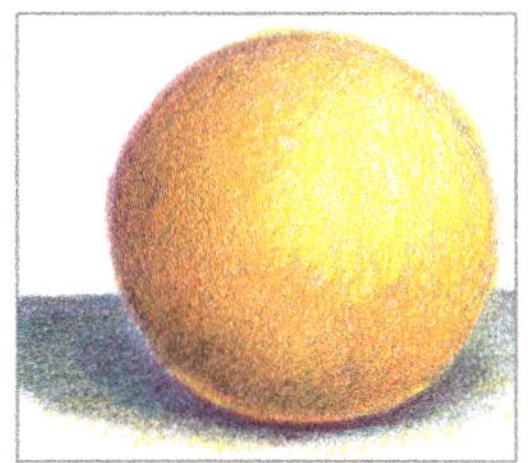

Building Depth Add the darkest values last. As the sphere curves away from the light, the values become darker, so place the darkest values on the side directly opposite the light.

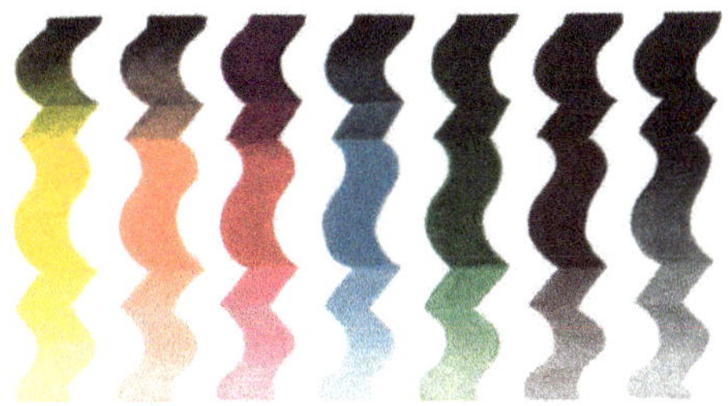

Color Values In this diagram each color was applied using graduated pressure—light, then heavy, then light. Then black was applied at the top and white was applied at the bottom to tint and tone the colors, respectively.

Tints, Shades, and Tones

Pure colors can be *tinted* with white to make them lighter, *shaded* with black to make them darker, or *toned* with gray to make them more muted. However adding a layer of black or white over a pure color might dull the color a bit. To revive some of the original intensity, go back over the tint or shade with the pure color. Also, to tint a color without muting it, try applying the white first and then adding the color over it.

Color Psychology

Colors are often referred to in terms of "temperature." An easy way to understand color temperature is to think of the color wheel as divided into two halves: The colors on the red side are warm; the colors on the blue side are cool. Thus, colors with red or yellow in them appear warmer, and colors with more green or blue in them appear cooler. For instance, if a normally cool color (like green) has more yellow added to it, it will appear warmer; and if a warm color (like red) has a little more blue, it will seem cooler. Additionally, warm colors appear to come forward, and cool colors appear to recede; this knowledge is valuable when creating the illusion of depth in a scene.

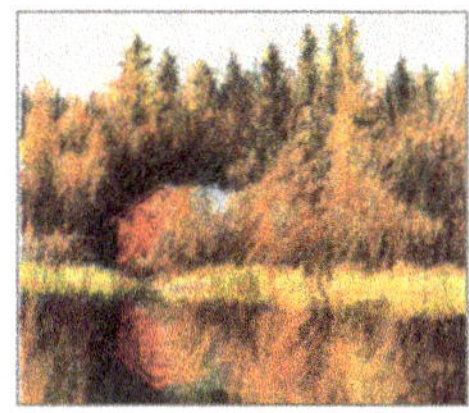

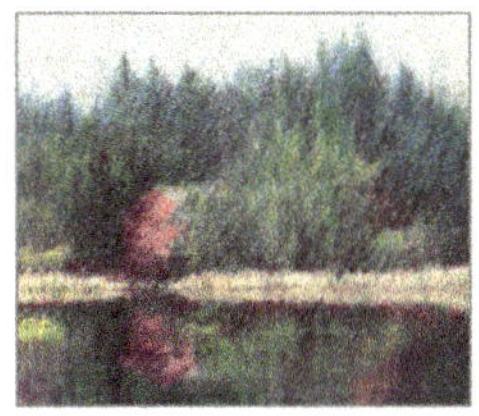

Warm Versus Cool Here the same scene is drawn with two different palettes: one warm (left) and one cool (right). Notice that the mood is strikingly different in each scene. This is because color arouses certain feelings; for example, warm colors generally convey energy and excitement, whereas cooler colors usually indicate peace and calm.

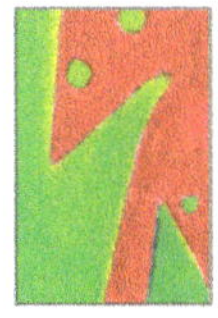

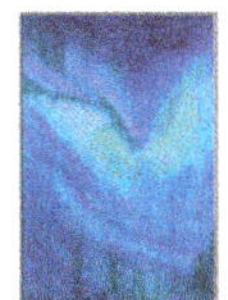

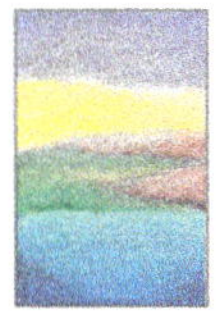

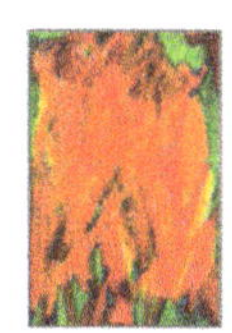

Color Mood The examples above further illustrate how color can be used to create mood (left to right): Complements can create a sense of tension; cool hues can evoke a sense of mystery; light, cool colors can provide a feeling of tranquility; and warm colors can create a sense of danger.

Colored Pencil Techniques

Colored pencil is satisfying to work with, partly because it's so easily manipulated and controlled. The way you sharpen your pencil, the way you hold it, and the amount of pressure you apply all affect the strokes you create. With colored pencils, you can create everything from soft blends to brilliant highlights to realistic textures. Once you get the basics down, you'll be able to decide which techniques will capture your subject's unique qualities. There are as many techniques in the art of colored pencil as there are effects—and the more you practice and experiment, the more potential you will see in the images that inspire you.

Strokes

Each line you make in a colored pencil drawing is important—and the direction, width, and texture of the line you draw will all contribute to the effects you create. Practice making different strokes, as shown in these examples. Apply light, medium, and heavy pressure; use the side and then the point of your pencil; and experiment with long, sweeping strokes as well as short, precise ones.

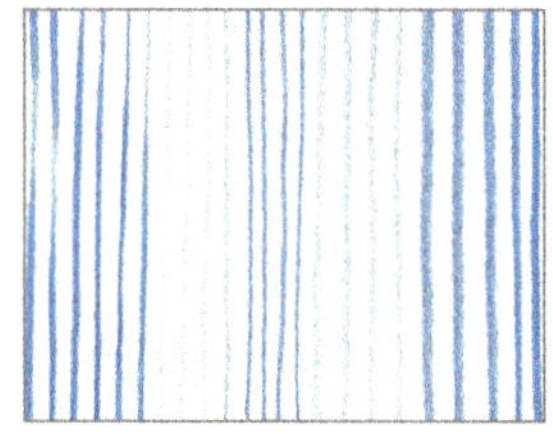

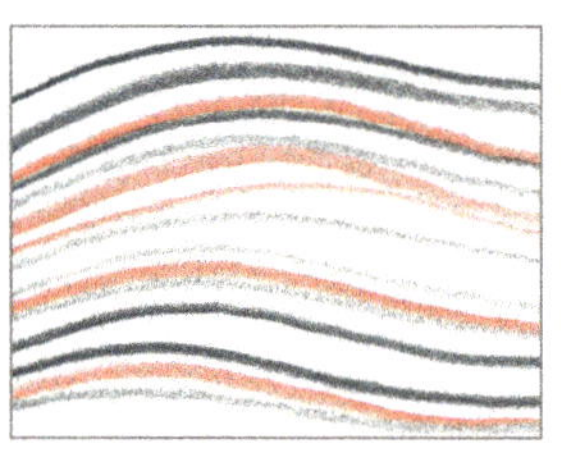

Strokes and Movement While a group of straight lines can suggest direction, a group of slightly curved lines conveys a sense of motion more clearly. Try combining a variety of strokes to create a busy design. Exercises like these can give you an idea of how the lines and strokes you draw can be expressive as well as descriptive.

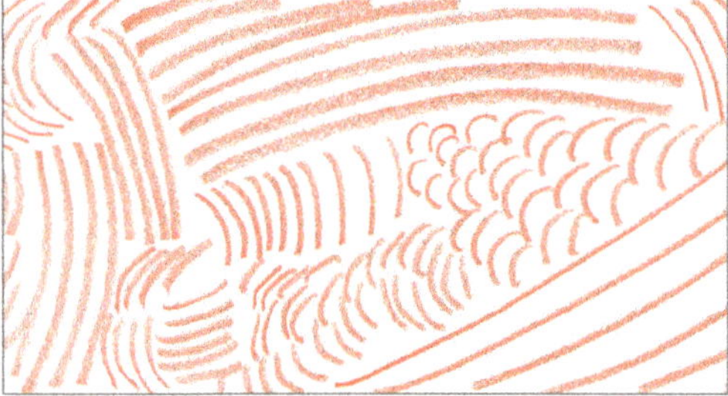

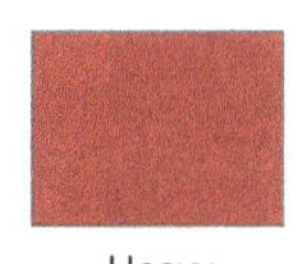

Light pressure | Medium pressure | Heavy pressure

Pressure Varying the amount of pressure you use on your pencil is an easy way to transition between values. Because colored pencils are translucent, the color of the paper underneath will show through. With light pressure, the color is almost transparent. Medium pressure creates a good foundation for layering. Heavy pressure flattens the paper texture, so color appears almost solid.

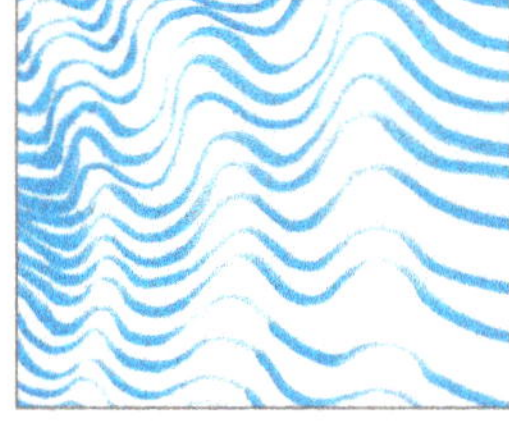

Varied Line Try varying the width and weight of the lines you create to make them more textured and interesting. These calligraphic lines can help create a feeling of dimension in your drawing.

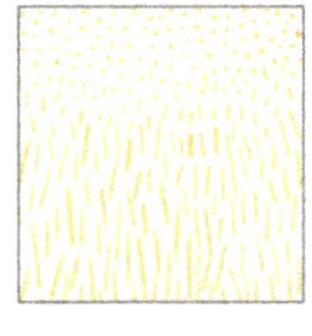

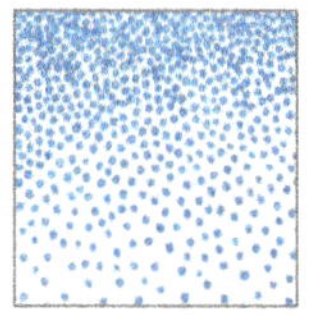

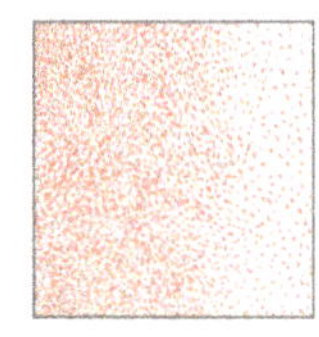

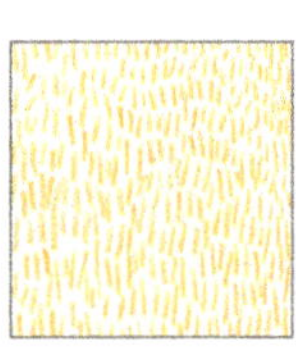

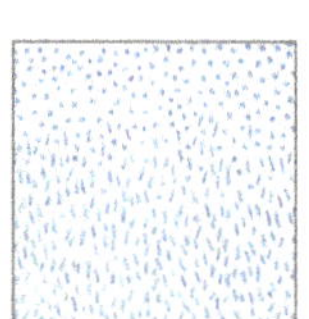

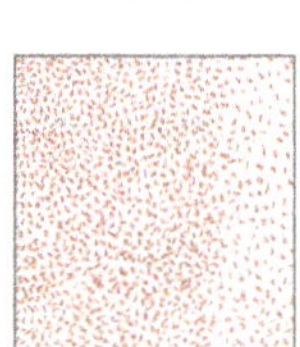

Strokes and Texture You can imitate a number of different textures by creating patterns of dots and dashes on the paper. To create dense, even dots, try twisting the point of your pencil on the paper.

Hatching

The term *hatching* refers to creating a series of roughly parallel lines. The density of color you create with hatch strokes depends on the weight of the lines you draw and how much space you leave between them. *Crosshatching* is laying one set of hatched lines over another but in the opposite direction, producing a meshlike pattern. Hatch and crosshatch strokes can both be used to fill in an almost solid area of color, or they can be used to create texture, as shown at right.

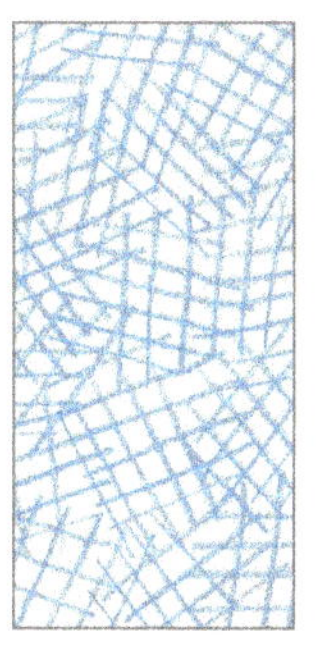
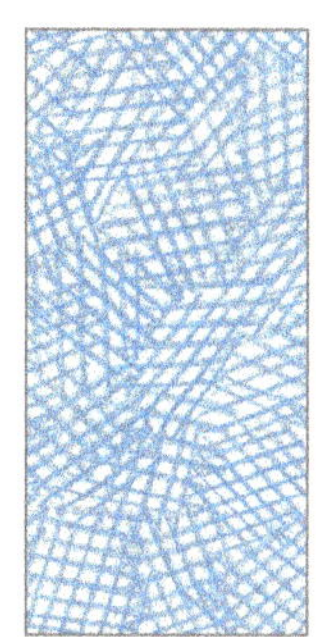
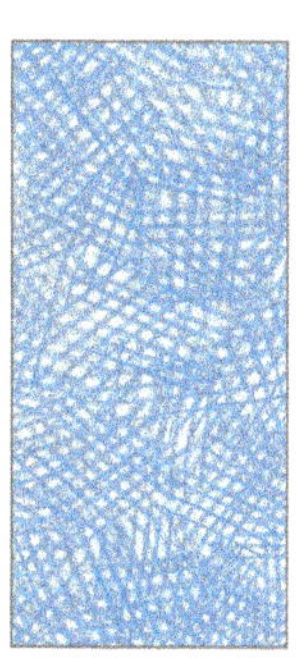

Cross-Hatched Spacing Filling in space with crosshatch strokes in random directions creates the dense, haphazard texture shown above. For a smoother, more even texture, crosshatch in two directions only (left leaning and right leaning).

Handling the Pencil

The way you hold the pencil impacts the strokes you create. Some grips will allow you to press more firmly, resulting in dark, dense strokes. Other grips hinder the amount of pressure you can apply, rendering lighter strokes. Still others give you greater control, allowing you to create fine details. Try each of the grips below, and choose those that are the most comfortable and create the effects you desire.

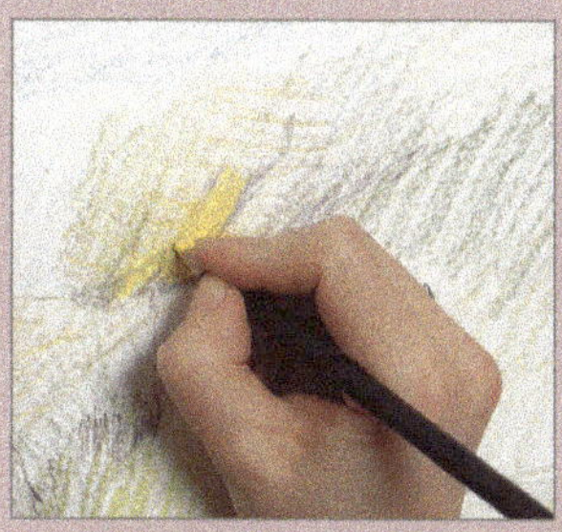
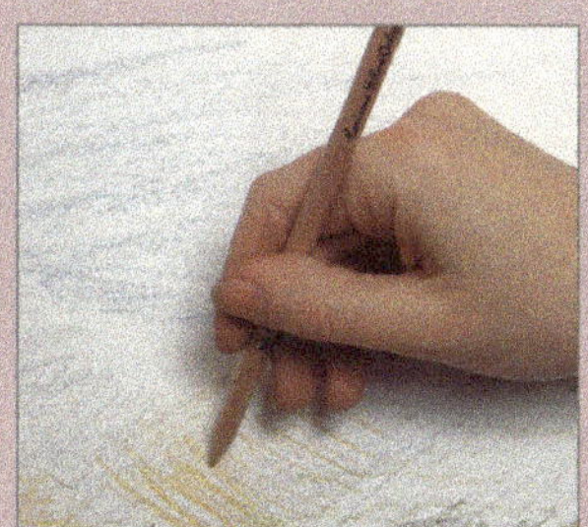

Conventional Grip For the most control, grasp the pencil about 1-1/2" from the tip. Hold it the same way you write, with the pencil resting firmly against your middle finger. This grip is perfect for smooth applications of color, as well as for making hatch strokes and small, circular strokes.

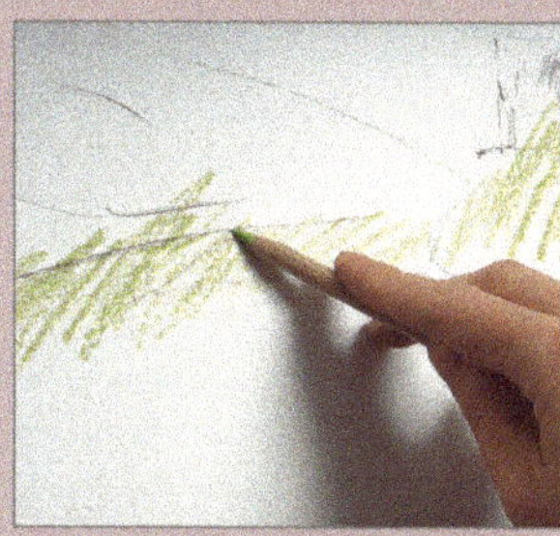

Overhand Grip Guide the pencil by laying your index finger along the shaft. This is the best grip for using heavy pressure.

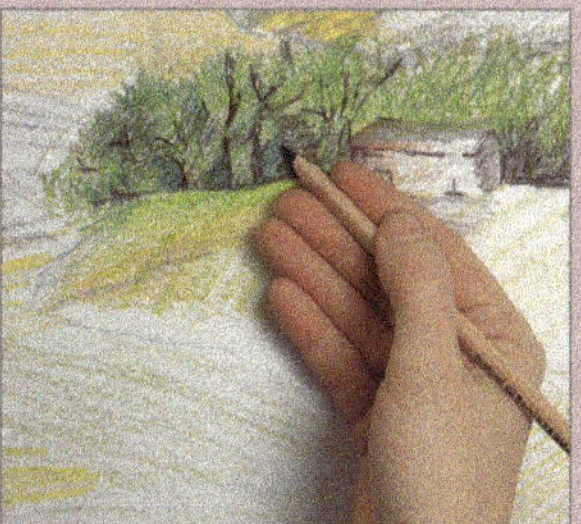
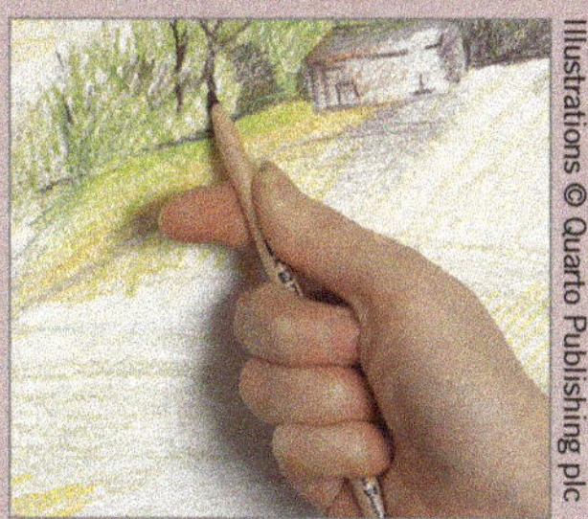

Underhand Grip When you cradle the pencil in your hand (as in either example shown above), you control it by applying pressure only with the thumb and index finger. This grip can produce a lighter line, but keep in mind that when you hold the pencil this way, your whole hand should move (not just your wrist and fingers).

Layering and Blending

Because colored pencils are translucent, artists use a transparent layering process to either build up color or create new hues. This layering process is wonderful because it creates a much richer hue than you could ever achieve if you were using just one pure color. To deepen a color, layer more of the same over it; to dull it, use its complement. If you want to blend your strokes together, you can use a colorless blender, as shown at the bottom of the page.

Layering with Hatch Strokes In the examples at right, yellow, orange, red, and blue were layered on top of one another with crosshatch strokes to demonstrate one way of creating a new color. To avoid getting a hue that's too dark, begin with the lightest color and work up to the darkest. This way you can tell if the mix is getting too muddy or deep.

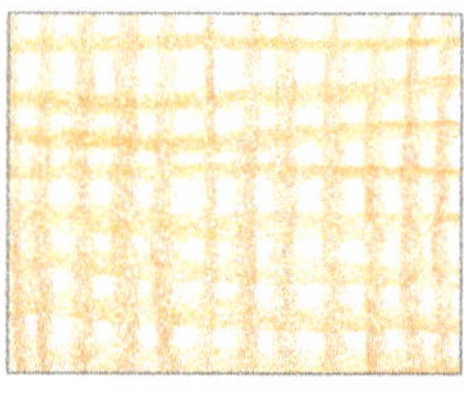
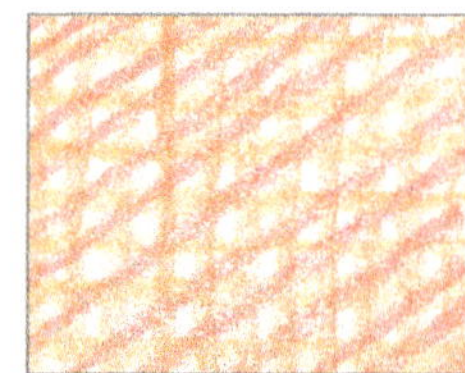
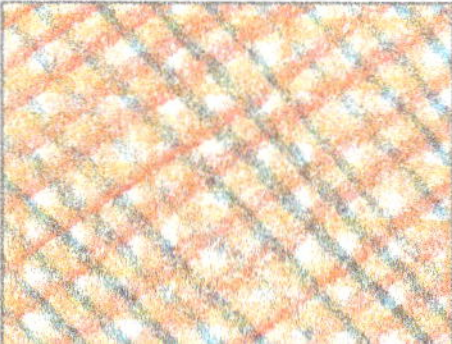
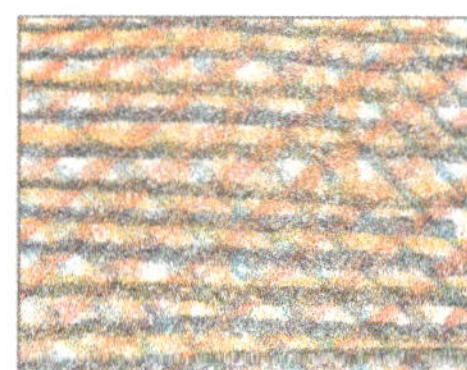
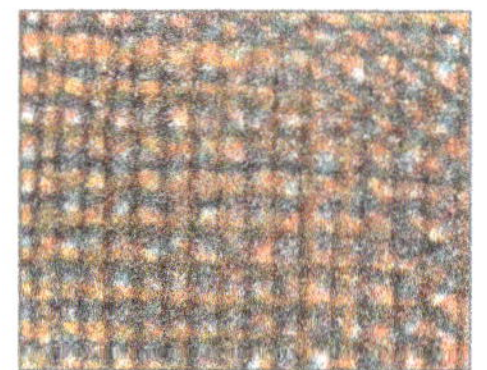

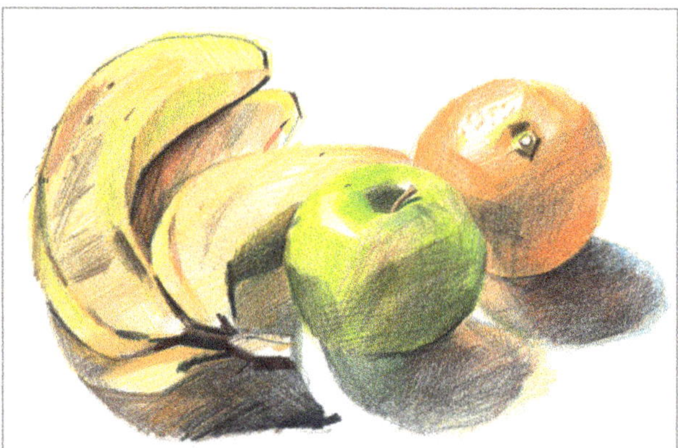

Building Up Color Here is a simple still life rendered with layers of hatch strokes. The forms of the fruit were built up by layering different values of the same color and then dulled a bit with a touch of their complements. Notice that the shadows under the fruit are blends of many different colors; they are never just gray or black.

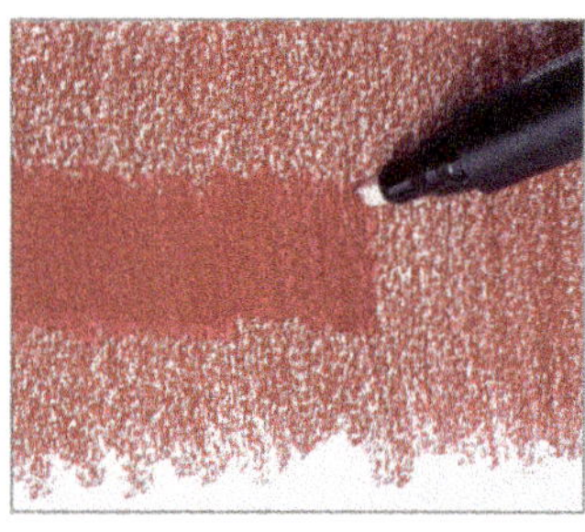

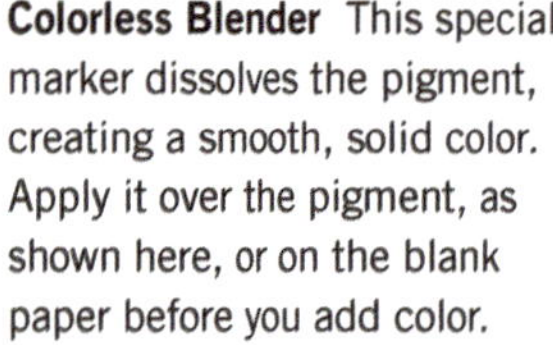

Colorless Blender This special marker dissolves the pigment, creating a smooth, solid color. Apply it over the pigment, as shown here, or on the blank paper before you add color.

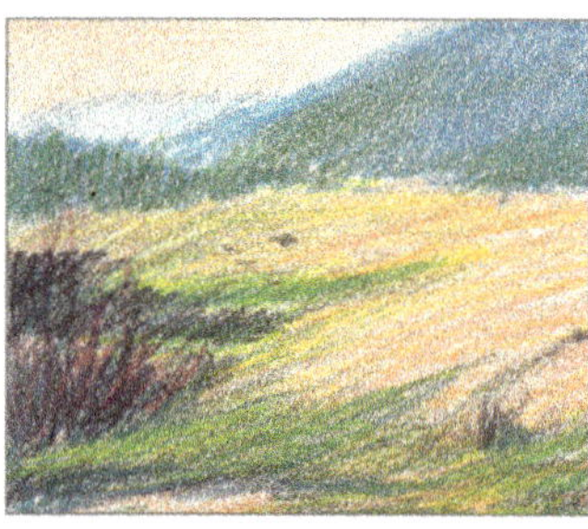
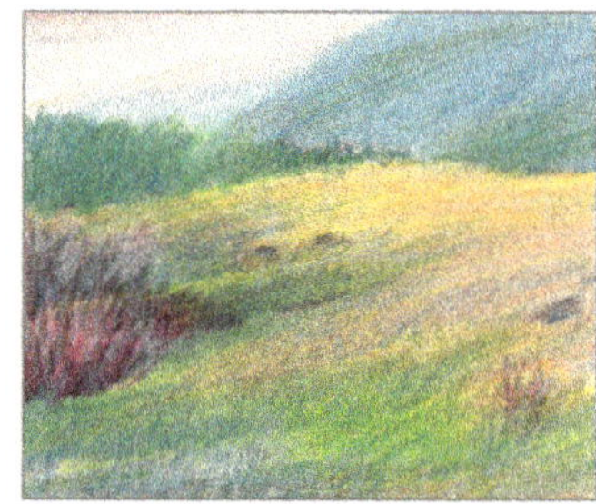

Using a Colorless Blender The example at left shows a quick study created with colored pencils. In the second example at right, a colorless blender was used to blend the pigments. Notice how much smoother the strokes appear after blending. The surface of the paper also becomes a little slick after using the blender, so any colors you add over the blended layer will glide easily on the page.

Burnishing

Burnishing (or opaque layering) is a blending technique that requires heavy pressure to meld two or more colors, which also flattens the tooth of the paper. Usually a heavy layer of white (or another light color) is applied over darker colors to create a smooth, shiny blend, as shown in the example below. Try not to press too hard on the underlayers of the area you intend to burnish; if you flatten the paper too soon, the resulting blend won't be as effective.

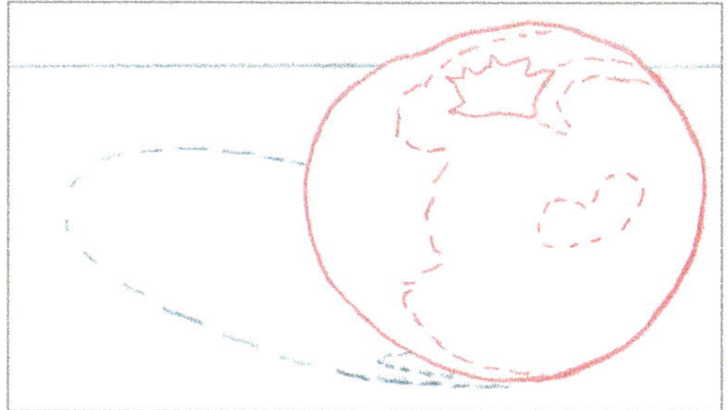

Step One Begin with a line drawing in *local color* (the actual color of the object) so the outline won't be visible when you're done. Press lightly so the outlines aren't impressed into the paper surface, creating dents. Here the solid lines indicate where hard edges will be, and the dashes or broken lines denote soft edges and shadows.

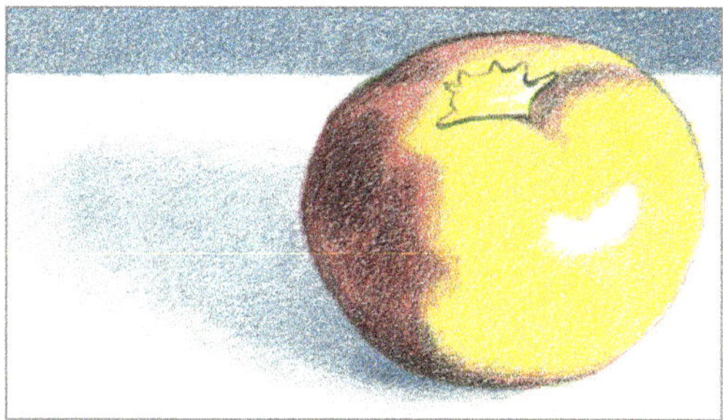

Step Two As you fill in the outlines with layers of color, keep the pencils sharp. Apply light to medium pressure as you slowly build color from light to dark. Use short, controlled strokes for a smooth tone, gradually lessening the pressure at the edges to make them soft. Here the darkest areas are created with green, the complement of red.

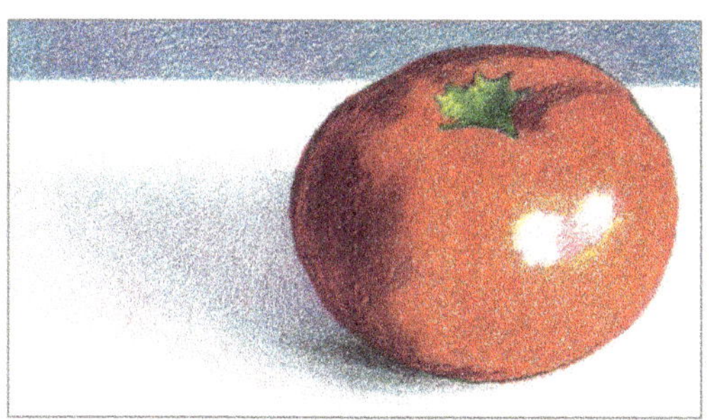

Step Three Next layer the different values of red and green, using heavier pressure. Be sure to fill in any highlights with white; this will act as a sort of barrier against saturation from the other colors.

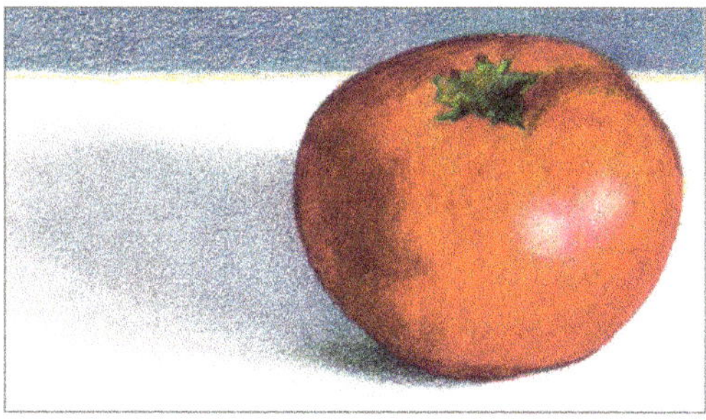

Step Four Finish by using a semi-sharp white pencil with circular strokes to burnish first the highlights and then the rest of the object. You may need to burnish over the same areas more than once to get an even blend.

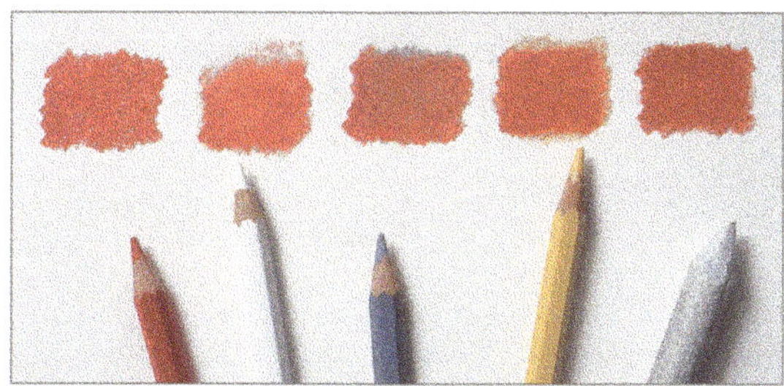

Effects of Burnishing Here various colors and techniques were used to burnish over the same red hue. At far left is the original, untouched color. To the right is shown the effect of burnishing with white, with blue, and with yellow, in that order. At far right, a blending stump was used to burnish the color. There are also colorless (without pigment) blending pencils available that many artists prefer—they are nontoxic and easy to use.

Special Effects and Techniques

As you're working in colored pencil, you may sometimes need to go beyond the basics and use some specialized techniques and materials, like the ones shown here. For example, you may choose to use black paper to provide a dramatic backdrop, lift off color with tape to reveal highlights, or make impressed lines to create texture. There are literally hundreds of possible techniques, so feel free to invent your own!

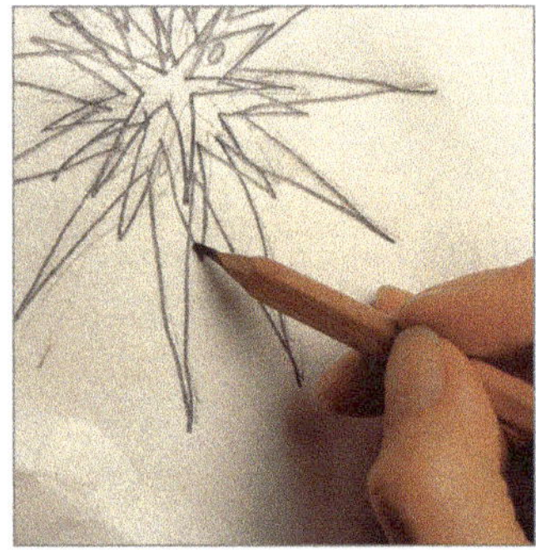

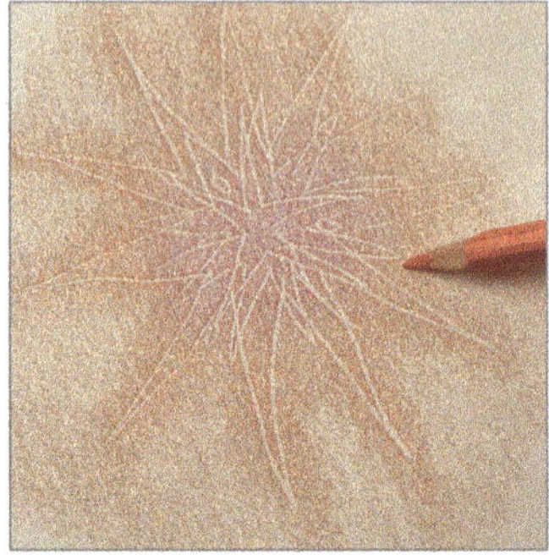

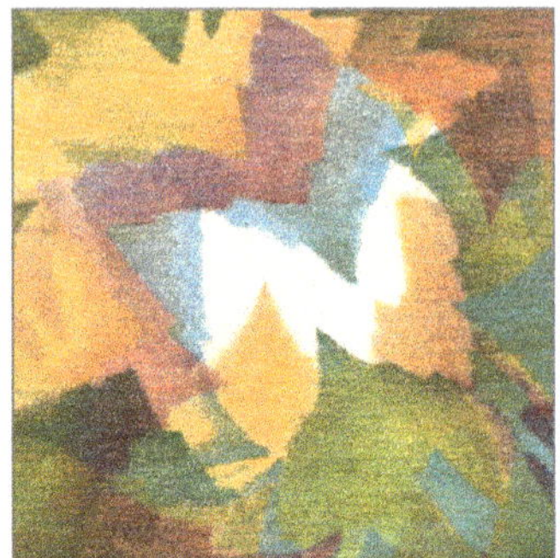

Impressed Line To resist color with an impressed line, draw a design on tracing paper, place it over your drawing paper, and trace over it firmly to leave an impression on the paper underneath. (You can also press lines directly into the paper with your fingernail or a stylus.) Then shade over the impressed lines, using the side of the pencil and light pressure to avoid filling in the lines completely.

Using Stencils For a stylized pattern, cut out a stencil and draw the shape repeatedly on your paper. For the pattern shown above, randomly fill in the shapes with a variety of colors.

Using Transparent Tape to Erase For soft highlights, such as the light line shown on the pencil at right, place transparent tape over the area. Then use a stylus to draw over the tape where you want to remove color. Carefully lift off the tape; then repair the spots where too much color was lifted. Try testing this on your paper before drawing, since some papers could be damaged by this technique. And if the tape removes too much color, stick the tape to your clothing first (to remove some of the tack) and then try again.

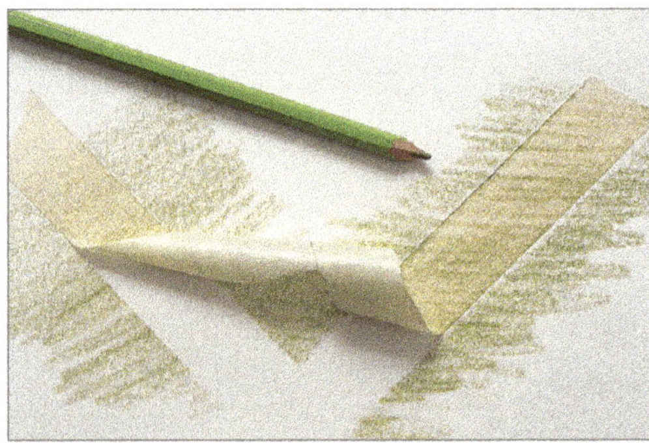

Masking with Tape You can use artist tape or masking tape to create clean lines and simple borders, as shown above. Just place the tape where you want it, apply color over it, and then remove it to reveal clean lines underneath.

Using Ink Using a fine-tipped, permanent marker is an interesting way to create dark values, as in this leaf. When you layer translucent pencil over the ink, the ink will show through, creating a darker value than you'd get with pencil alone. Just be sure to use a smudge-proof marker so it won't smear on your drawing paper.

Frottage Rubbing over a textured surface, like the leaf at right, with the side of a pencil is a technique called "frottage." This creates an impression of the object (and its texture) on your paper.

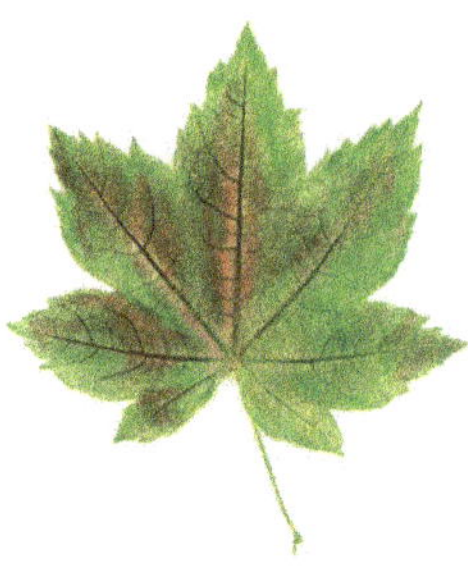

Watersoluble Pencils

Watersoluble, or watercolor, pencils offer the same amount of control and detail as regular colored pencils, but they have the added versatility of being similar to painting tools as well. When you blend them with a brush and water, the artwork you create will have a softer, more painterly effect.

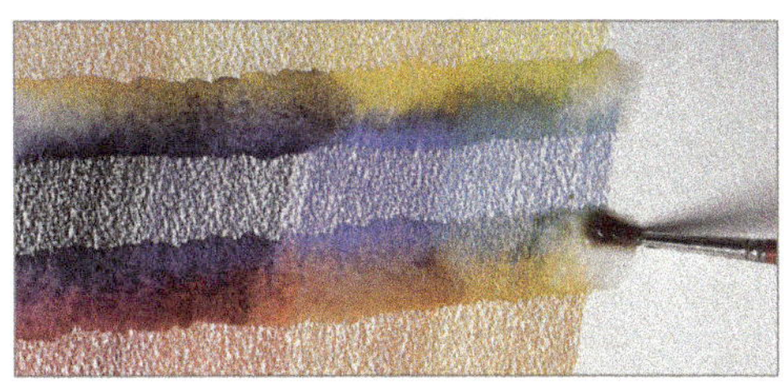

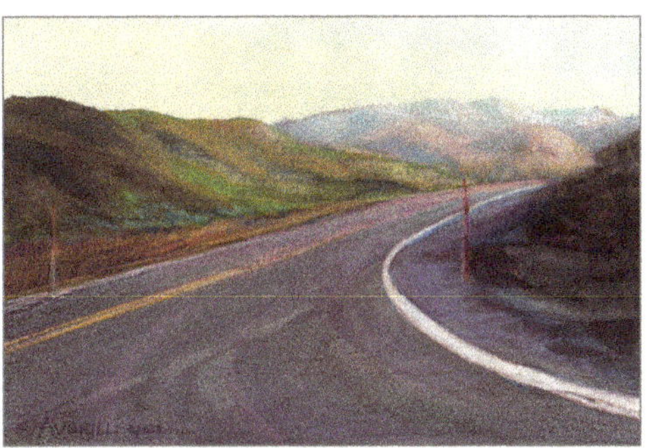

Watersoluble Pencil You can blend watersoluble pencils with a wet brush (top) to create soft blends like the ones shown in the sky, in the hills, and on the road (bottom).

Special Papers

You can also use colored grounds, multimedia panels, illustration boards, and specialty papers (such as velour, sandpaper, or mylar) for your drawings. Each will give you a different result—some offer more texture or provide an undercolor, and others are better suited for mixed-media projects. When choosing paper, make sure you select one of high quality, and test out the pencils and techniques you plan to use ahead of time.

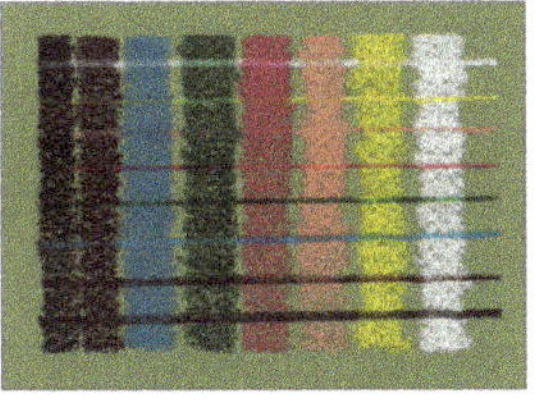

Colored Grounds If you choose a colored support that shares a dominant hue in your drawing, you can create harmony among the colors in your drawing and save a significant amount of time—the paper provides a medium value to build color on (see example at right). Make a test sheet first on the back of your paper (or on a scrap piece of paper, as shown above) to see how the colors in your palette will be affected by the colored ground you choose.

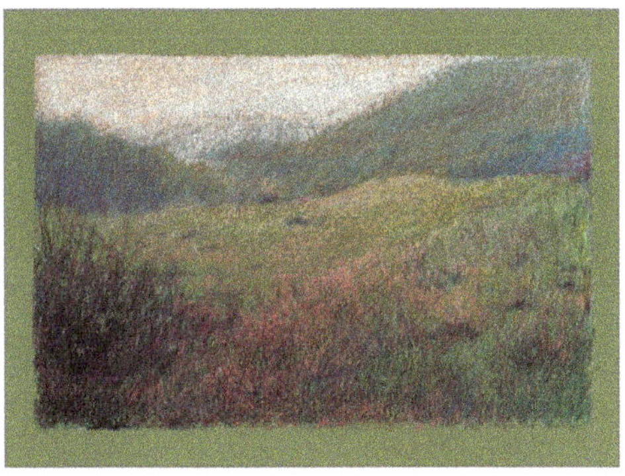

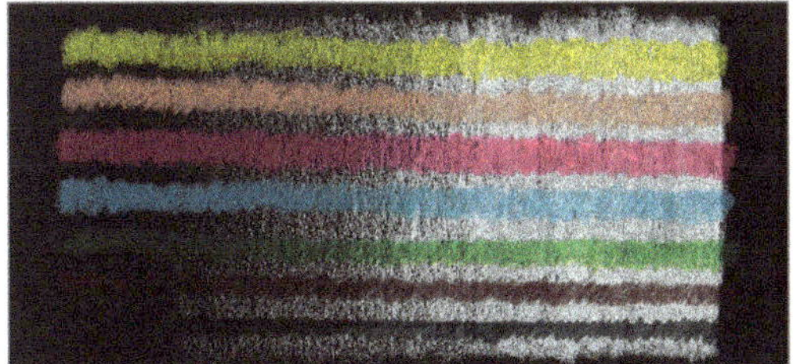

Black Paper The contrast of light colors on black paper creates a sense of drama. Bright, colorful subjects appear even bolder over a dark ground. For the most brilliant hues, apply a layer of white before applying color over it.

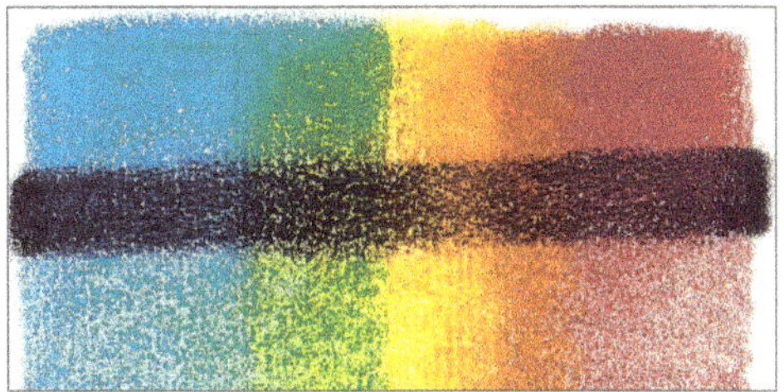

Sanded Paper "Sanded paper" has a gritty quality to it that lends an interesting texture to colored pencil art. The rough surface will sand off the point of your pencil, so make sure to keep a dust brush handy to sweep away the residue.

About the Artists

Debra Kauffman Yaun

A graduate of the Ringling School of Art and Design in Sarasota, Florida, Debra Yaun began her art career as a fashion illustrator and graphic designer. Later she discovered a book on colored pencil in a library and fell in love with the medium. Now she stays busy with portrait commissions and nature drawings. As time allows, she teaches an occasional art class. Her artwork has been published in several art magazines and books, and Debra is a juried member of the Portrait Society of Atlanta, where she serves on the board of directors. She is also a member of the Colored Pencil Society of America.

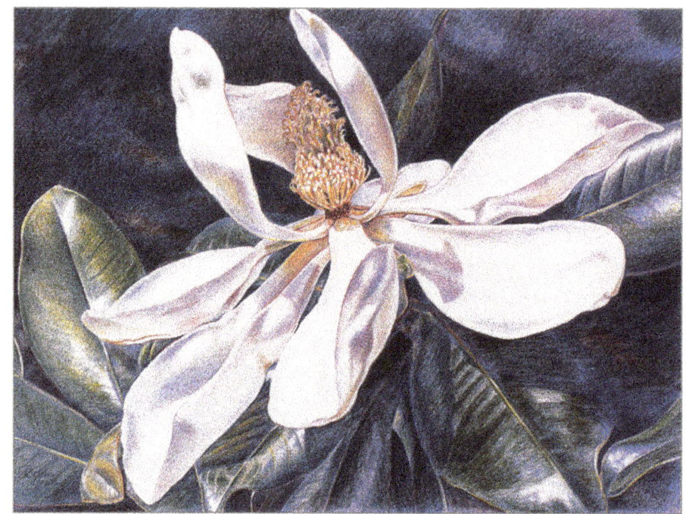

Pat Averill

Although she considers herself primarily self-taught, Pat Averill has attended an array of workshops and seminars on oil, watercolor, and colored pencil. She considers the way she figuratively "inhales" the colors, values, and shapes she observes around her to be an integral part of her artistic process. To her, the creation of art is based on a combination of life experiences and the artist's reaction to the subject matter. Pat is a charter member of the Colored Pencil Society of America, and she has won numerous awards in juried international exhibitions for her work in colored pencil.

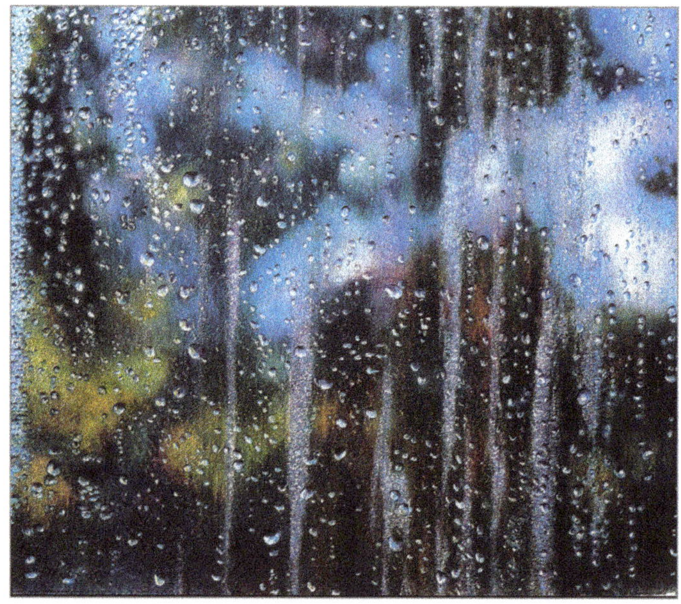

Sylvester Hickmon, Jr.

Native South Carolinian Sylvester Hickmon, Jr., became interested in art at an early age. He received his formal art training at South Carolina State University, Orangeburg, where he earned a Bachelor of Science in Art Education. For the past 13 years, he has taught art at the high school, middle school, and elementary school levels. He also conducts workshops on drawing with colored pencil. Sylvester has exhibited throughout the United States, and his works can be found in many private collections. He has also received numerous regional awards and national recognition for his colored pencil art. Sylvester is a signature member of the Colored Pencil Society of America, a member of the Sumter Artists' Guild, and serves on the Board of Directors of the Sumter Gallery of Art.

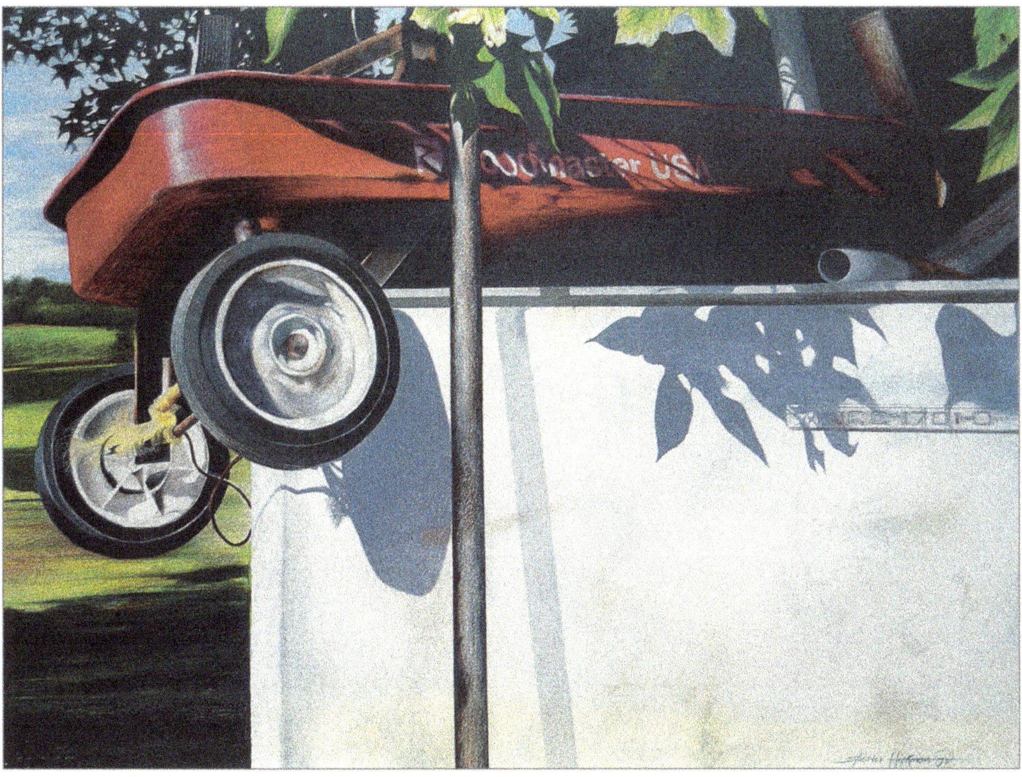

Color Palettes

Most artists have a group of favorite colors and brands they prefer working with; below are the colors used for the projects in this book. Keep in mind that the names of the colors may vary among brands. Sometimes two pencils that have the same name are two different hues. The colors shown here are for general color reference only. Although great care has been taken in the production of this book, the printing process has limitations, so some colors cannot be replicated with complete accuracy.

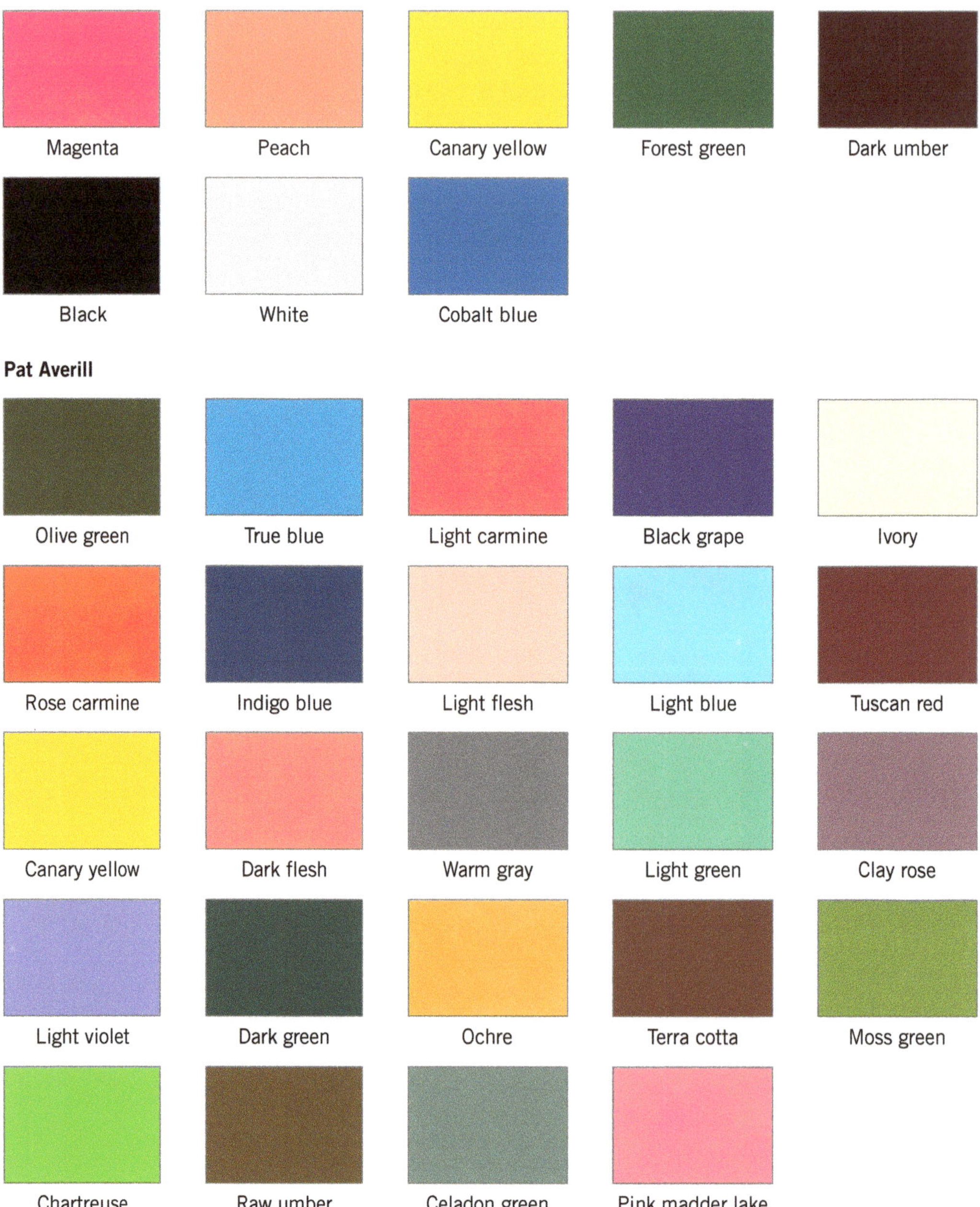

Sylvester Hickmon

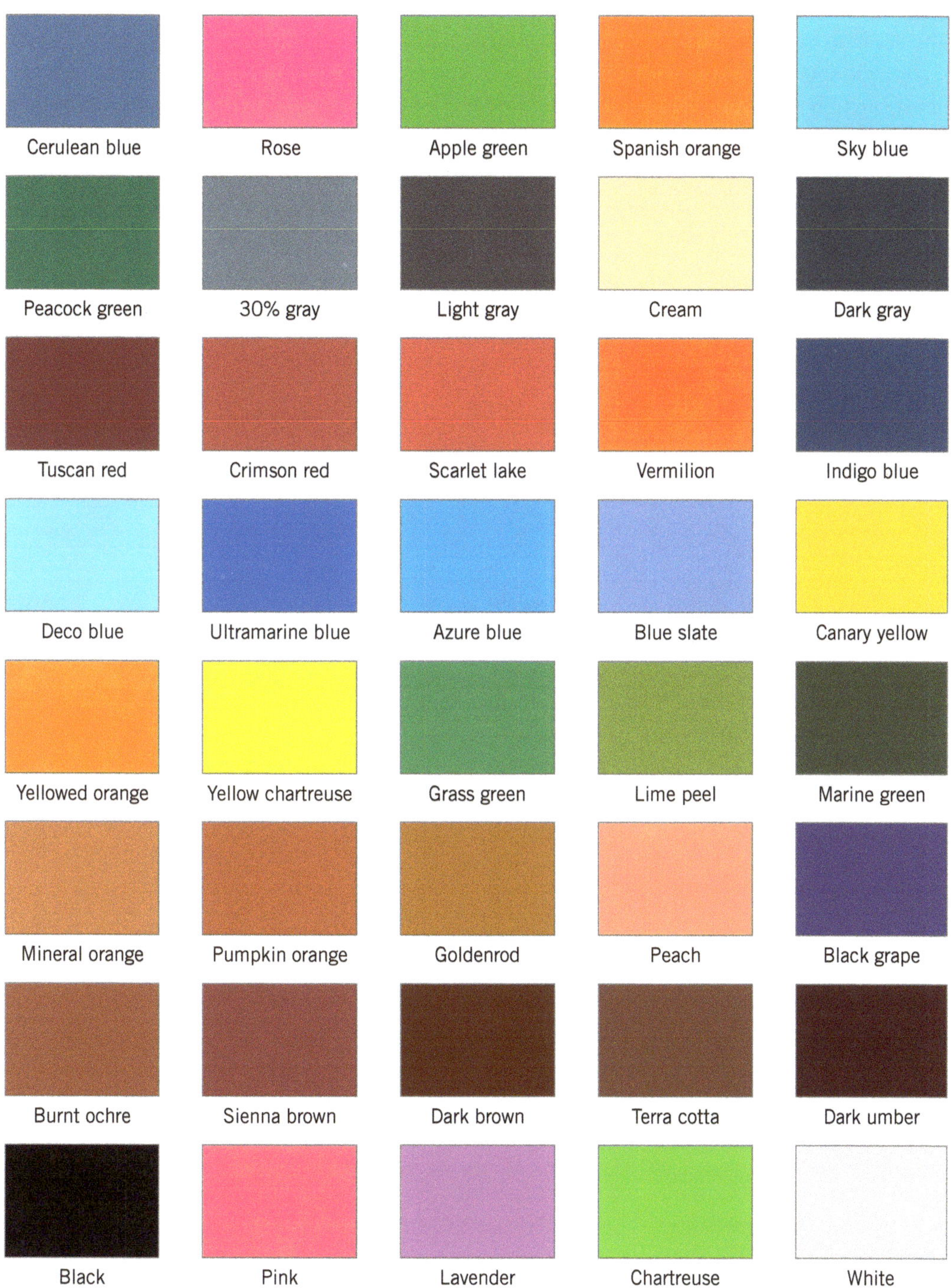

Making the Best of a Limited Palette with Debra Yaun

An artist may choose a *limited palette* (just a few colors) for convenience, experimentation, or the desire to express a particular mood in a scene (such as using only blues and greens to depict a somber mood). Working with a limited palette can also force you to think creatively—you must carefully plan your values, blend and build up colors that you don't have in your palette, and use special techniques to achieve the effects you want. It's certainly simpler to depict a colorful subject with a huge selection of colors, but consider challenging yourself by working with a limited palette. In this example (and in all of her lessons in this book), Debra Yaun admirably extracts an amazing array of brilliant hues from only eight colors.

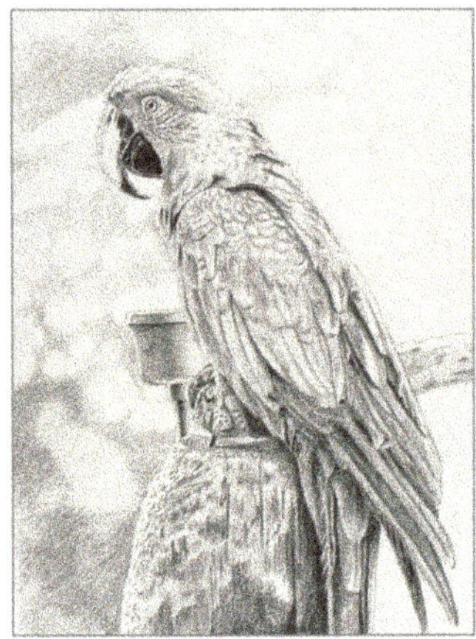

Step One I start with a sketch on practice paper, and then I transfer the drawing to my art paper. To do this, I cover the back with graphite (creating a sort of carbon paper). Then I place the drawing, graphite-side down, over my art paper and trace over the lines, effectively transferring the sketch to my drawing paper. Now I'm ready for color. I fill in the darkest areas first, using small, circular strokes of black colored pencil and smoothly applying the color to the feathers and the beak. I also use black for the shadows of the feet, the cup, and the perch, leaving some white along the edges to indicate the strong back lighting. Then I apply black in the background, forming some abstract shapes with smooth, circular strokes.

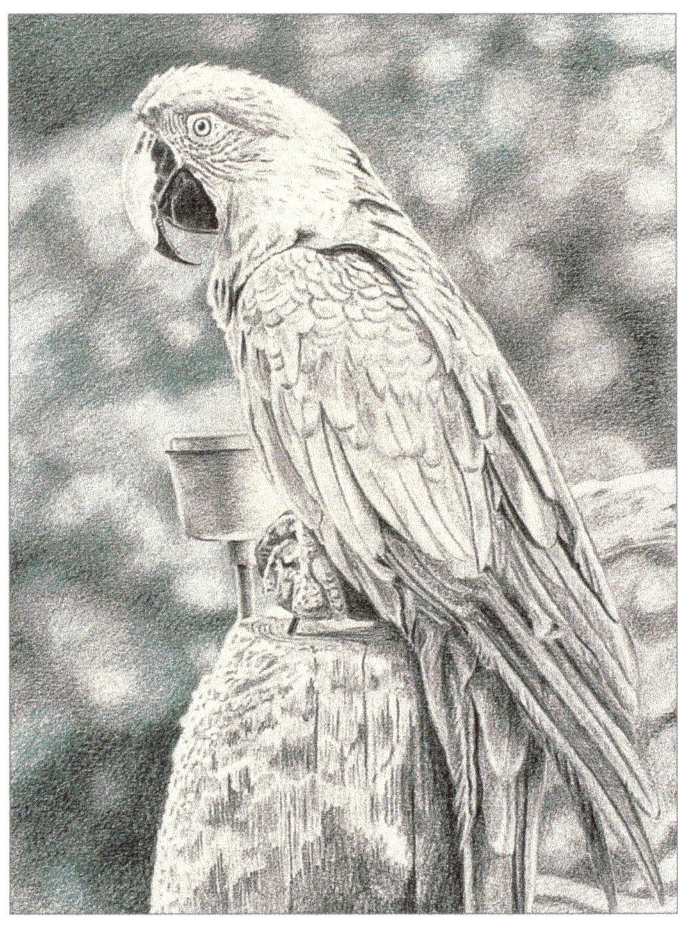

Step Two I darken the background with more black, adjusting the shapes for balance and interest but keeping them blurred so they don't compete with the subject. Then I apply a layer of cobalt blue over the black with circular strokes to keep the layers soft.

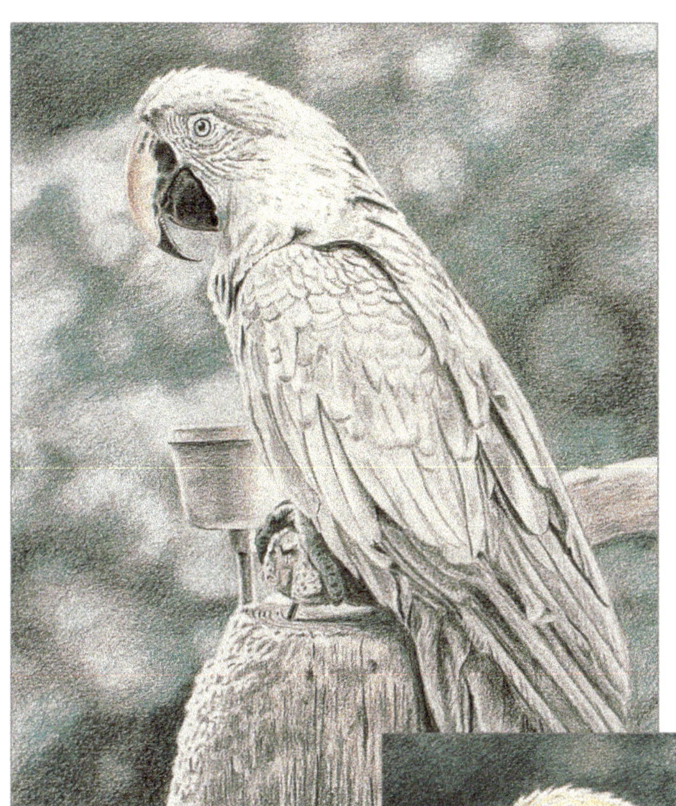

Step Three I add a little more cobalt blue to the background, to the iris of the eye, around the outside of the eye, and along the white area near the beak. I also apply blue with medium pressure over the black parts of the beak and feet and add blue to the bird's cast shadow. Then I stroke peach on the upper beak with a smooth, circular motion, leaving the white highlight at the outer edge. I also add some peach to the black areas of the beak to create small, cracklike lines. Then I apply peach lightly and smoothly to the cup, the wood perch, and the wood support, leaving the highlights white. I darken the wood a bit more with some black, using strokes that follow the direction of the wood grain.

Step Four I smoothly apply canary yellow to the beak, over the peach, using medium pressure. Then I add yellow to the head, the details around the eye, the chest, the top part of the wing, and the back. I layer some cobalt blue over the more shadowed areas of the head and over the black lines in the feathers. Next I lightly apply yellow to the cup, overlapping the white area a little. I also layer yellow over all the wood and on some of the light spots in the background. Then I apply dark green to the background, pressing firmly in small, circular motions over the darker areas. I make sure to keep my pencils sharp to help work the color into the paper. Then, using a blending stump, I soften the background colors with small, circular motions.

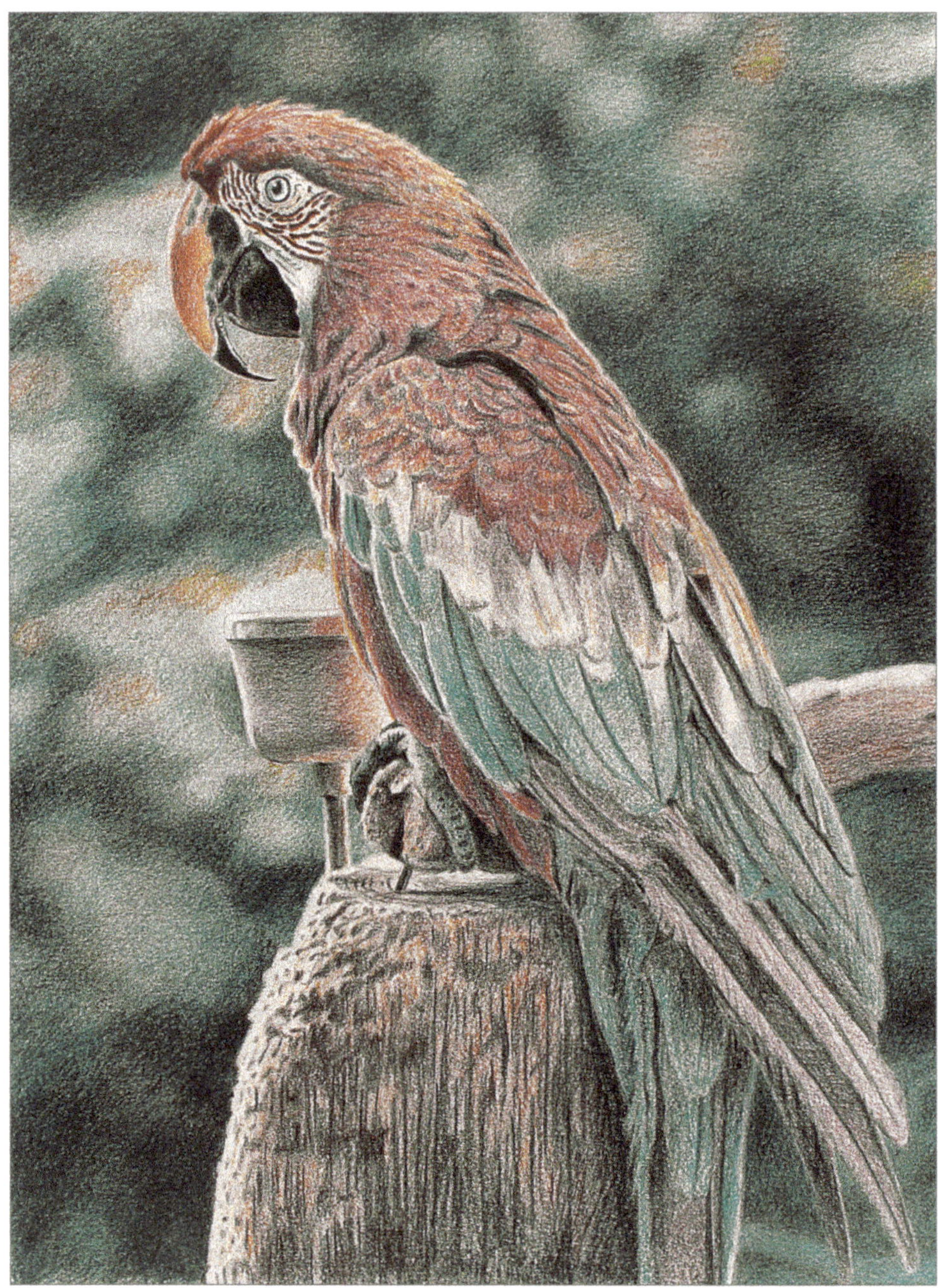

Step Five I apply first dark umber and then canary yellow to the perch with short, vertical strokes that mimic the wood grain. I also give the cup a light layer of dark umber, but I leave the edges white to indicate reflections of the strong sunlight. Since I don't have red in the limited palette I'm using, I must build a red hue by repeatedly layering magenta and yellow over each other. I begin with a layer of magenta to the head, using medium pressure and short strokes that follow the direction the feathers lie and allowing the yellow to show through along the top of the sunlit head. Next I apply magenta firmly to the spots on the face and under the eye, and then I go over the spots with a little more yellow to create an orange-red. I lightly add a little magenta on the beak and apply a layer of cobalt blue to a lower row of feathers, pressing firmly. Then I blend the feathers with the blending stump and add light layers of magenta and blue to the long wing and tail feathers.

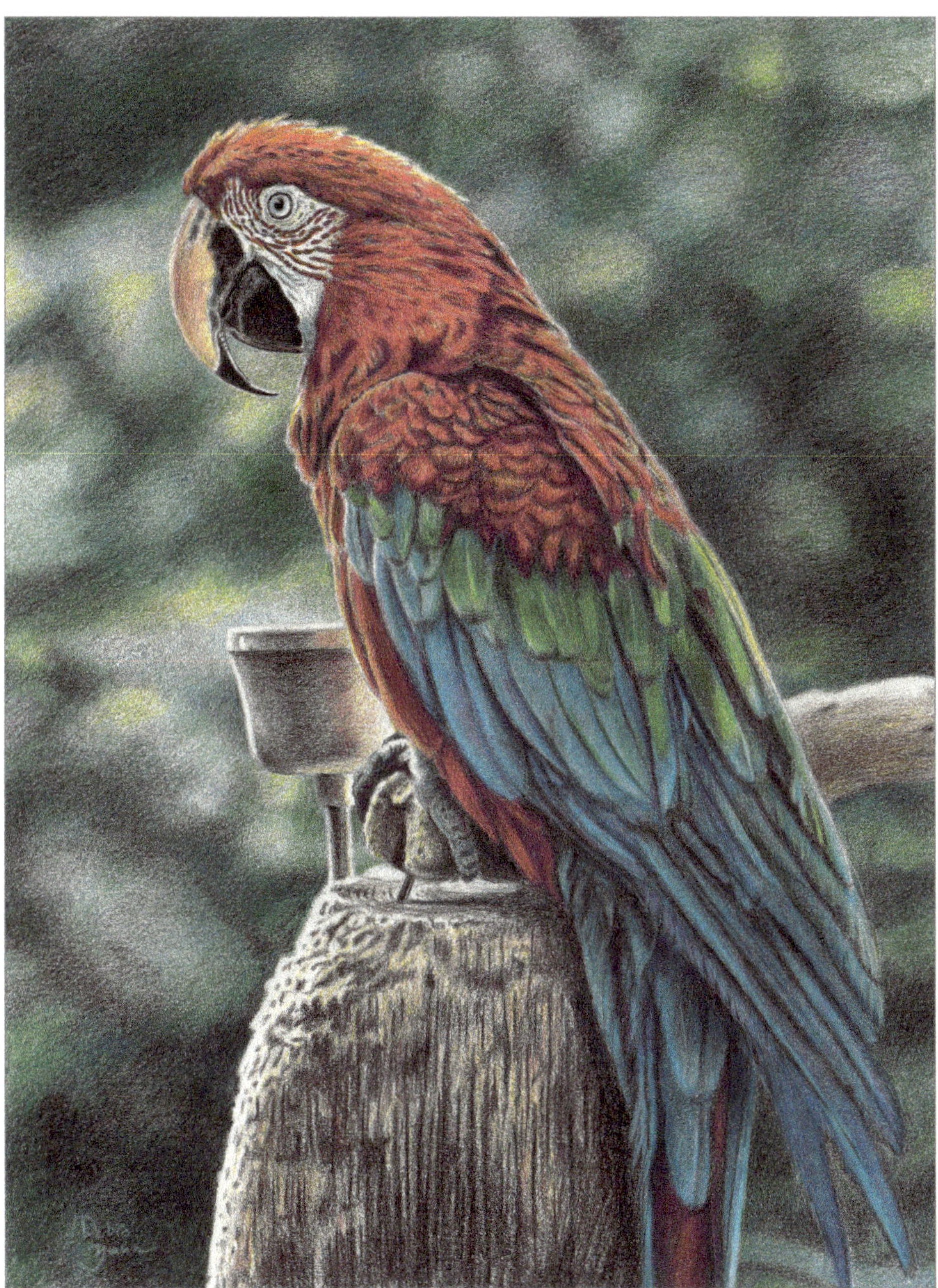

Step Six Next I apply first dark green and then canary yellow to the middle row of feathers. I layer more magenta on the head, and then I add white to a few areas to create lighter feathers on top. I add magenta to the cup to create the reflection and add a little more black to the center of the cup to give it some dimension. To balance the dark green behind the parrot's head, I add some dark umber in a circular motion. Then I use cobalt blue to smooth and blend the colors in the background and in the feathers. I use a blending stump to work in the color, and I apply white over the blue, pressing firmly to create some shine on the feathers. I use black to emphasize the edges of the tail feathers and blend it in with a blending stump. I lightly work magenta into some of the dark areas of the blue feathers and the one red tail feather, and I darken the edges of the red feathers with dark umber and black. Finally I add highlights with touches of white over the blue tail feathers.

Starting with a Simple Subject with Debra Yaun

Intricate, complex scenes are certainly visually interesting, but they can also be challenging to draw. A better way to begin is to choose a simple subject, which can be equally compelling, even with a limited palette. Before you start drawing, look closely at your subject and try to break it down into basic shapes (such as circles, triangles, and wedges). You can also reduce the distractions in your scene by keeping the background vague, as Debra Yaun did here in this simple portrayal of colorful daylilies.

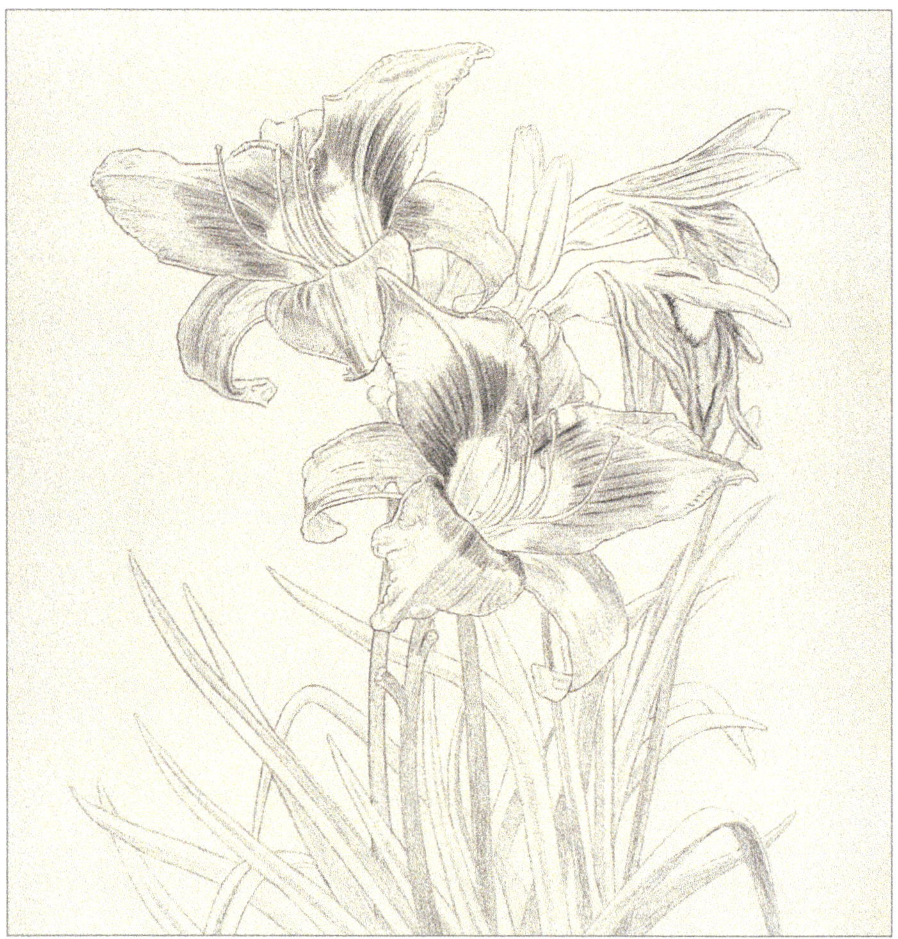

Step One First I sketch out the day lilies in graphite pencil, taking care to draw the correct proportions. Then I use black colored pencil to indicate the darkest veins on the flower petals, creating long strokes that start at the center of each flower. I am using a *grisaille* technique here (see page 33), applying black colored pencil to the stems and leaves with short, even strokes. This will establish a foundation for all the subsequent values in the drawing.

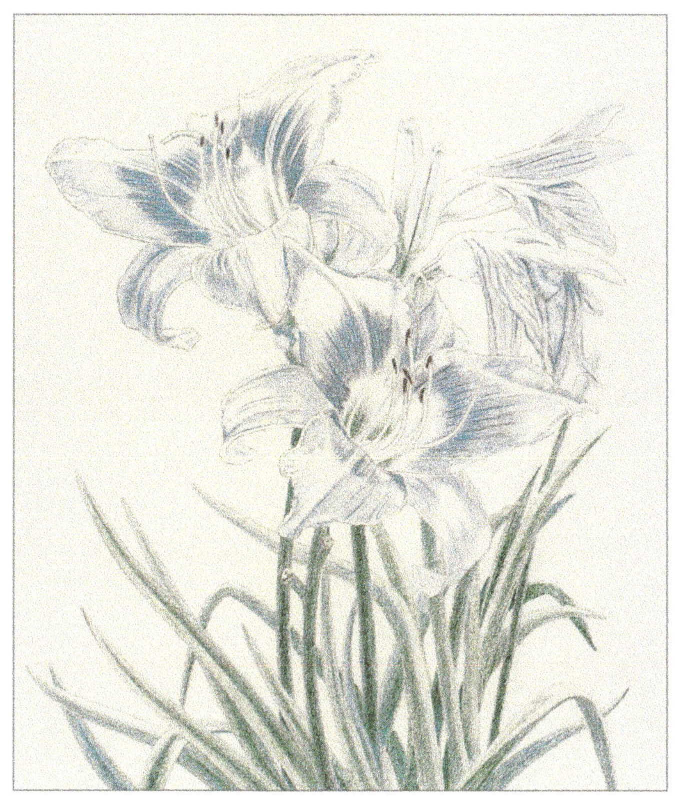

Step Two Next I lightly apply short strokes of cobalt blue over the black on the leaves. I also layer blue over the rest of the leaves, but I retain some of the white of my paper on the leaves in the foreground. This helps set the background leaves behind the foreground leaves. I give the stems a little heavier application of blue, since they appear a bit darker in my reference photo.

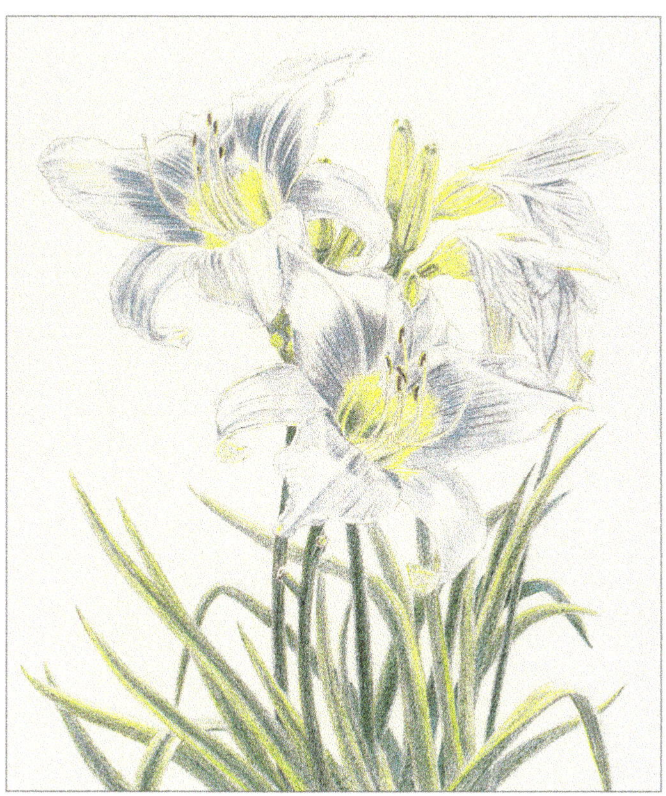

Step Three With short strokes, I add a light layer of dark green to the centers of the two open flowers. Then I apply dark umber to the ends of the stamens, leaving the pollen edges white. I use short strokes of dark green along the length of the leaves and stems, and then I lightly layer dark green on the flower buds and the bases of the two closed flowers. Next I add dark umber to the stems and some of the darker leaves and layer canary yellow over the green buds and leaves, using a paper stump to blend the colors. Then I apply more yellow to the leaves in the foreground. (Remember that warm colors appear to "pop" forward.) I layer black on the base of the stamen to indicate the shadow and apply a fairly heavy layer of yellow to the centers of the flowers. Then I use a sharp yellow pencil to indicate pollen on the stamens, leaving a white edge for contrast.

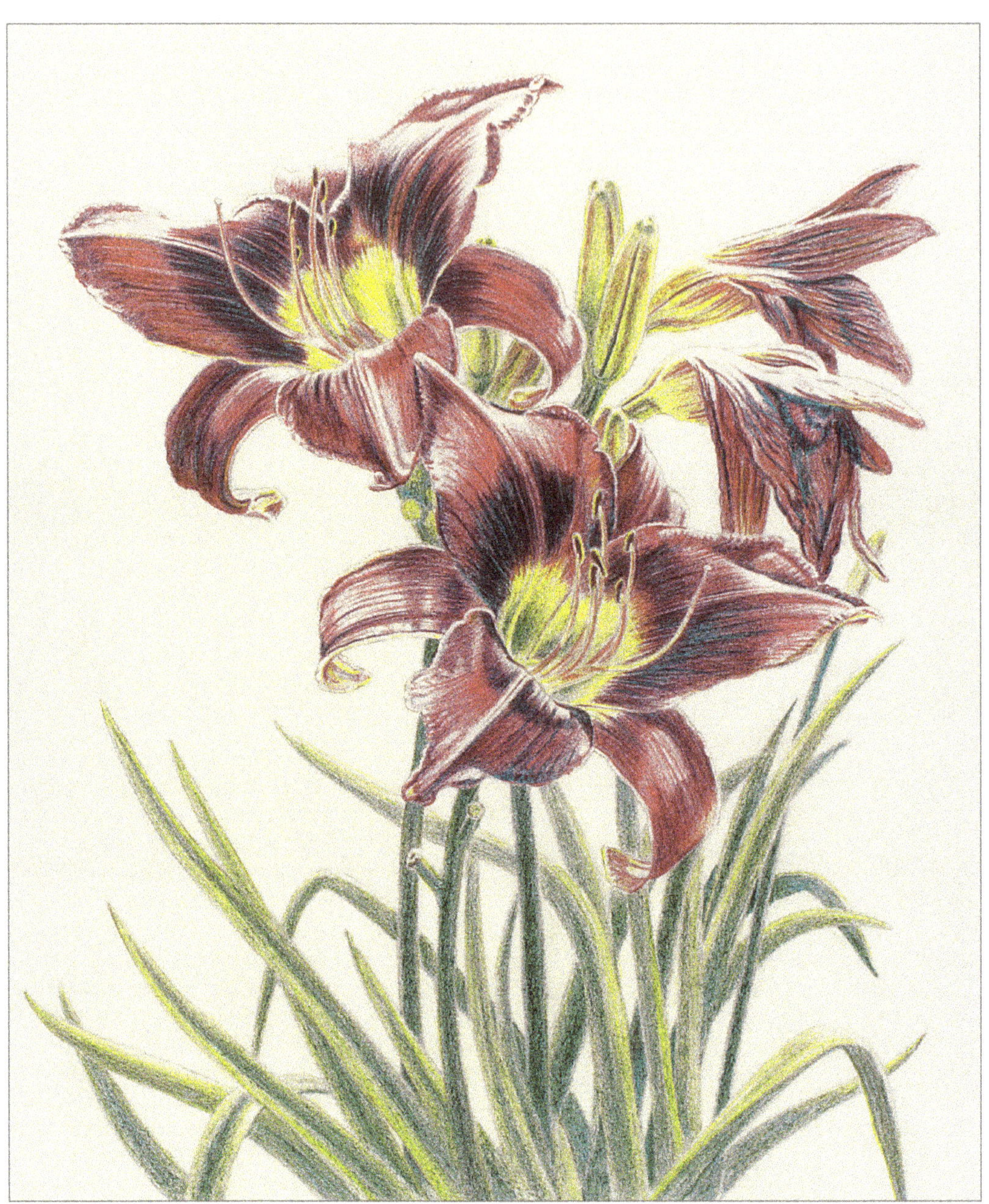

Step Four Using strokes that follow the direction of the veins, I add a layer of magenta to the open petals, leaving some white to indicate the sunlit areas. To achieve a "glow" on the petals, I layer magenta over the yellow to create orange; notice also that the cobalt blue I've added shows through under the magenta, creating a purple hue. Developing this variety of reds gives a better contrast between the shadows and the lighter areas. Next I lightly apply magenta along the petal lines and inner edges of the buds to indicate some reflected color from the surrounding flowers. I give the closed flowers a layer of magenta as well, pressing firmly where the petals fold. Then I layer magenta over the brown on the ends of the stamens to darken and warm them.

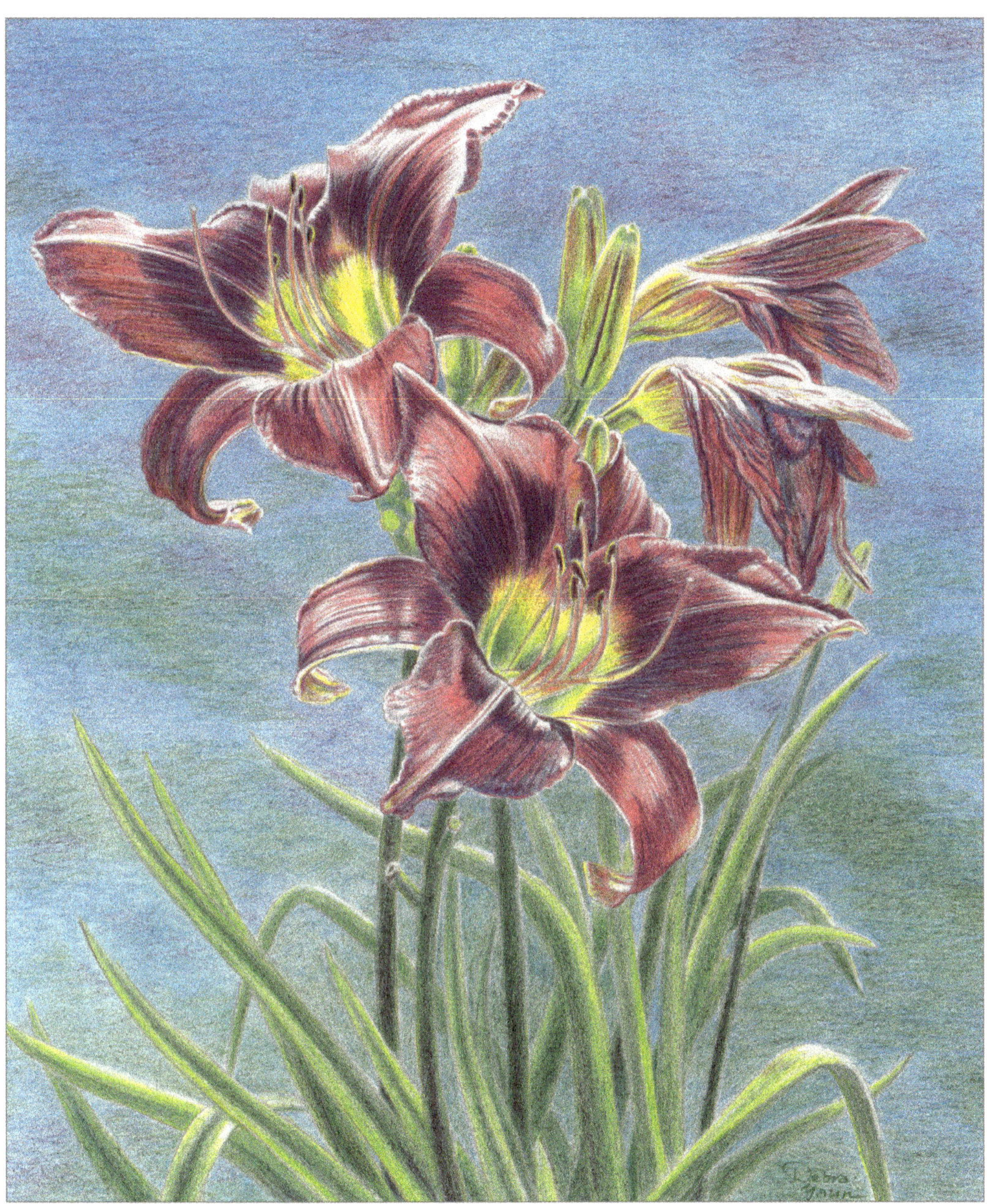

Step Five Next I erase any graphite lines that are still visible along the outside of the petals. Using medium pressure, I apply a layer of cobalt blue to the background with horizontal strokes. I keep the point of the pencil very sharp and stroke along the edges of the petals. Then I layer dark green and magenta onto the blue in horizontal strokes to add some color and interest to the background. Next I use a paper blending stump to soften and blend the background colors; I want to make sure I don't have a complex or distracting backdrop that would detract from these simple flowers. Finally I take another look at the leaves and decide they seem a little light, so I darken them in a few areas with some blue and more dark green.

Using References

with Debra Yaun

Observing nature firsthand is a wonderful practice for an artist. Be sure to bring a sketchbook with you so you can make some field sketches on site—these quick studies can be invaluable reference tools when you return to your studio. If you bring your camera along, you have the option of observing and recording a subject from several different angles. You can also snap various shots of the entire setting, as well as some closeups of the details. Give yourself as much information to work with as you can. When you return to the studio, you can compile your photos into a permanent file for future use. In this example, Debra Yaun portrays a colorful floral scene using a photo from her reference file.

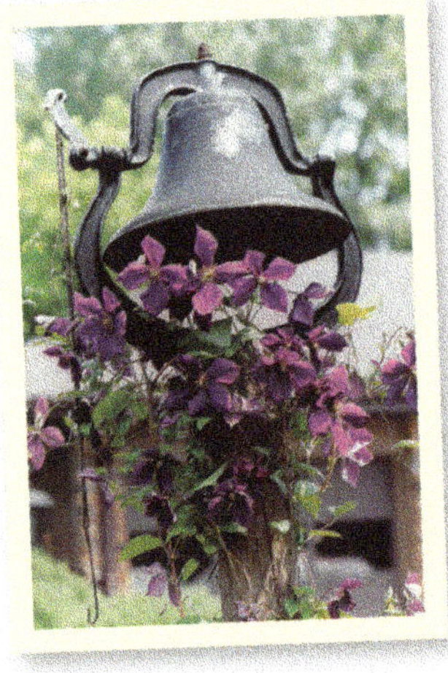

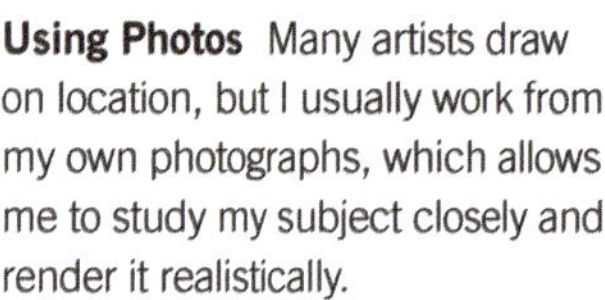

Using Photos Many artists draw on location, but I usually work from my own photographs, which allows me to study my subject closely and render it realistically.

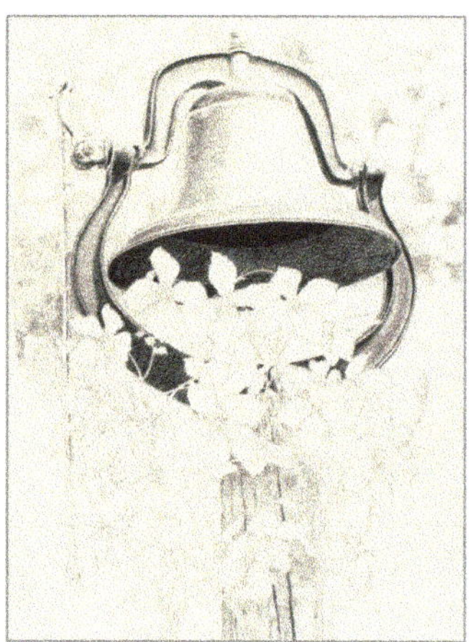

Step One I use a grid method to draw the bell and flowers to make sure I transfer the proportions correctly. I draw a grid onto a small piece of tracing paper and place it over the photo; then I draw a proportionate grid on my drawing paper and copy the lines from each square. I simplify the drawing by leaving out a few flowers and vines and omit the wire that wraps around the post. Then I apply black colored pencil to the darkest shadows of the bell and post and add a heavy layer of black to the center of the bell.

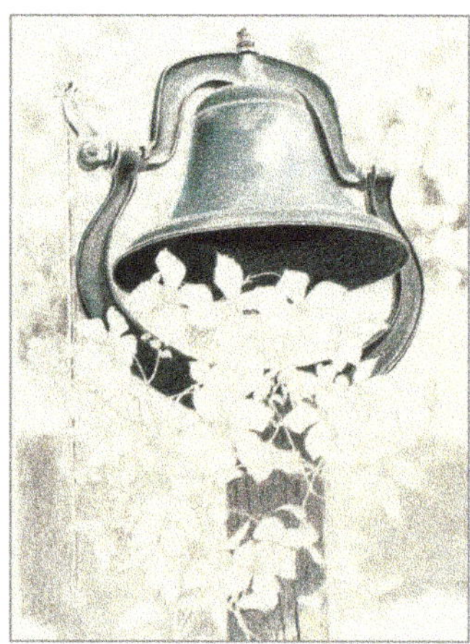

Step Two I apply a light layer of black to the background with small, circular strokes. I add a light layer of cobalt blue to the bell and the metal stand (over the black) to create a cool gray. I draw the blue out past the black onto the paper, leaving some white areas to indicate highlights. I apply blue to the darker areas of the post to "push" it back into shadows. I use vertical strokes to add a light layer of dark umber over the whole post, and then I lightly apply canary yellow to the bottom of the post.

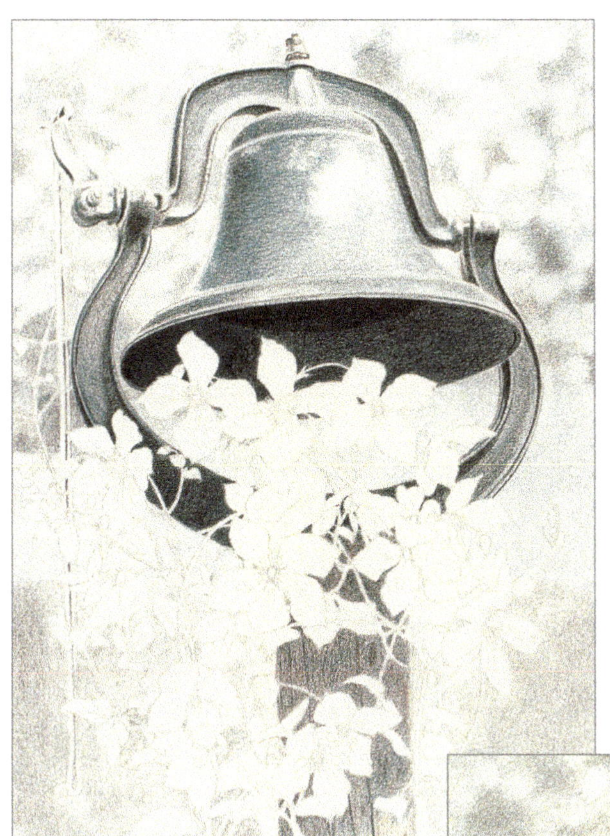

Step Three I add cobalt blue over the center and upper portions of the background, using light, circular strokes. Then I add black to the lower part of the background and blend it in with a blending stump. I simplify this area of the background to focus attention on the flowering vine. At the bottom of the paper, I add a layer of blue and then dark green to the background to vaguely represent foliage.

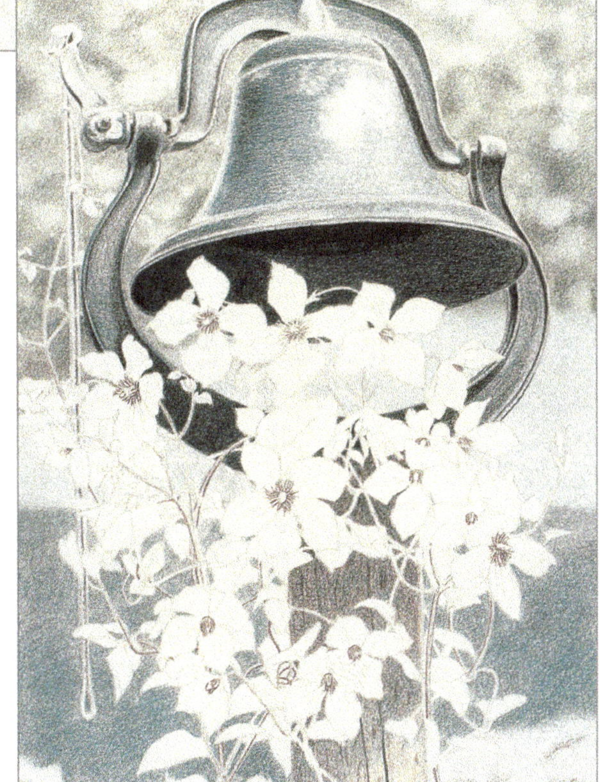

Step Four Next I layer dark umber in a few areas over the blue in the lower background, also outlining the centers of the flowers and the larger stems. Then I add a little cobalt blue shading to a few leaves and the rope, and I layer dark green over the background at the top. I apply dark umber to the nuts and bolts on top of the bell and handle and soften the light blue area in the middle of the bell with a blending stump. Pressing firmly, I give the bottom of the background a layer of blue and smooth it with a blending stump. Then I layer white over the blue in the middle background, and I layer canary yellow over the existing colors in the upper background to brighten the green values. I lightly add black to the flowers, indicating the lines in the petals and the shadows. Next I add dark green to the background at the bottom and blend it in with a blending stump. Then I layer blue over some areas of the background to build up more color.

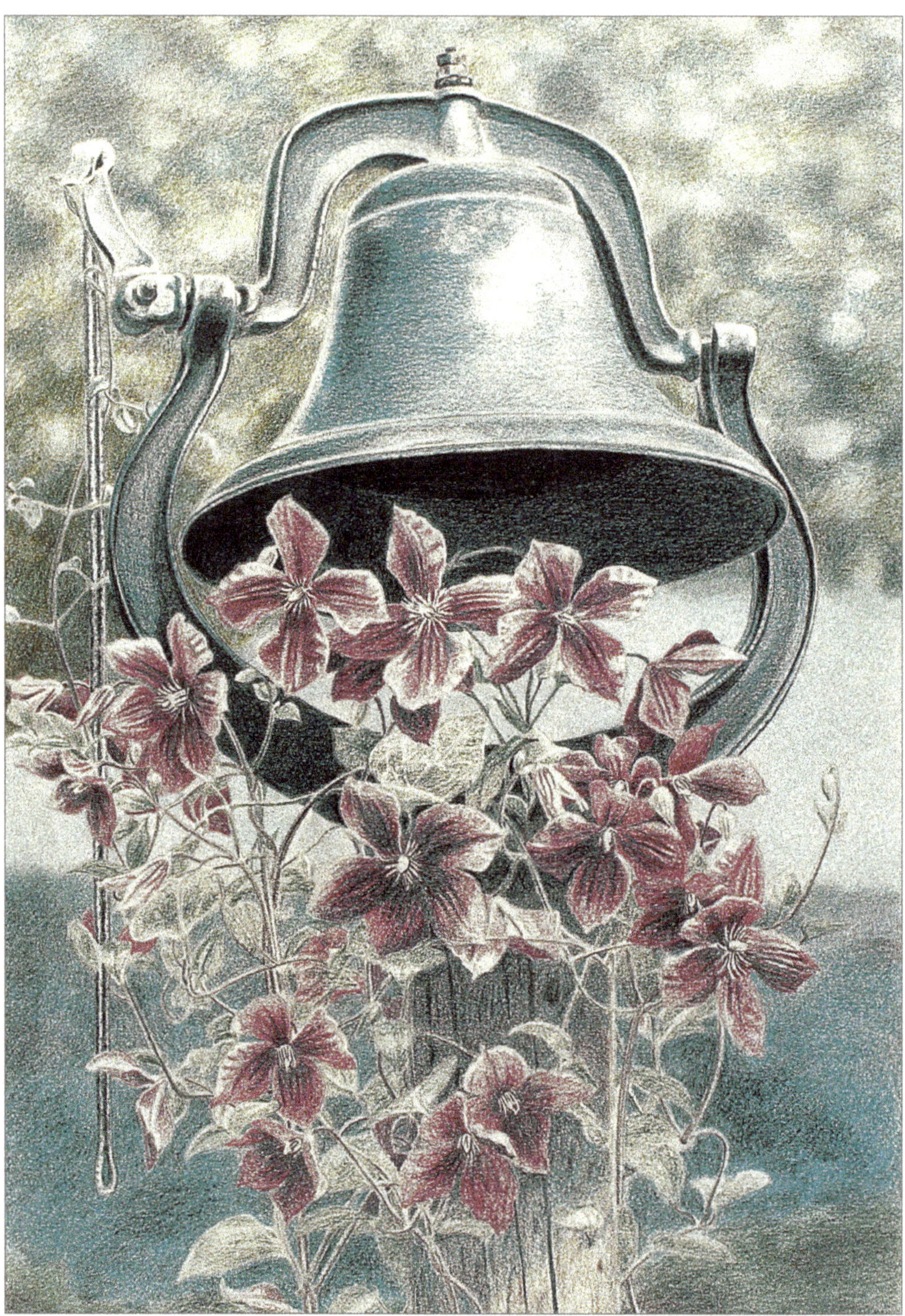

Step Five I sharpen my dark green pencil and add some detail to the leaves. Using medium pressure, I apply dark umber to more stems and layer magenta over the black lines and the shading on the petals. I leave the petal highlights white, but I add a little black to a few of the petals to darken them. I don't have the exact color of the petals in the limited palette I'm using here, but I can create it with layers of magenta, blue, and black. I use small circular strokes of black over the background at the bottom to darken it, and I add black to the bellpull to give it more dimension.

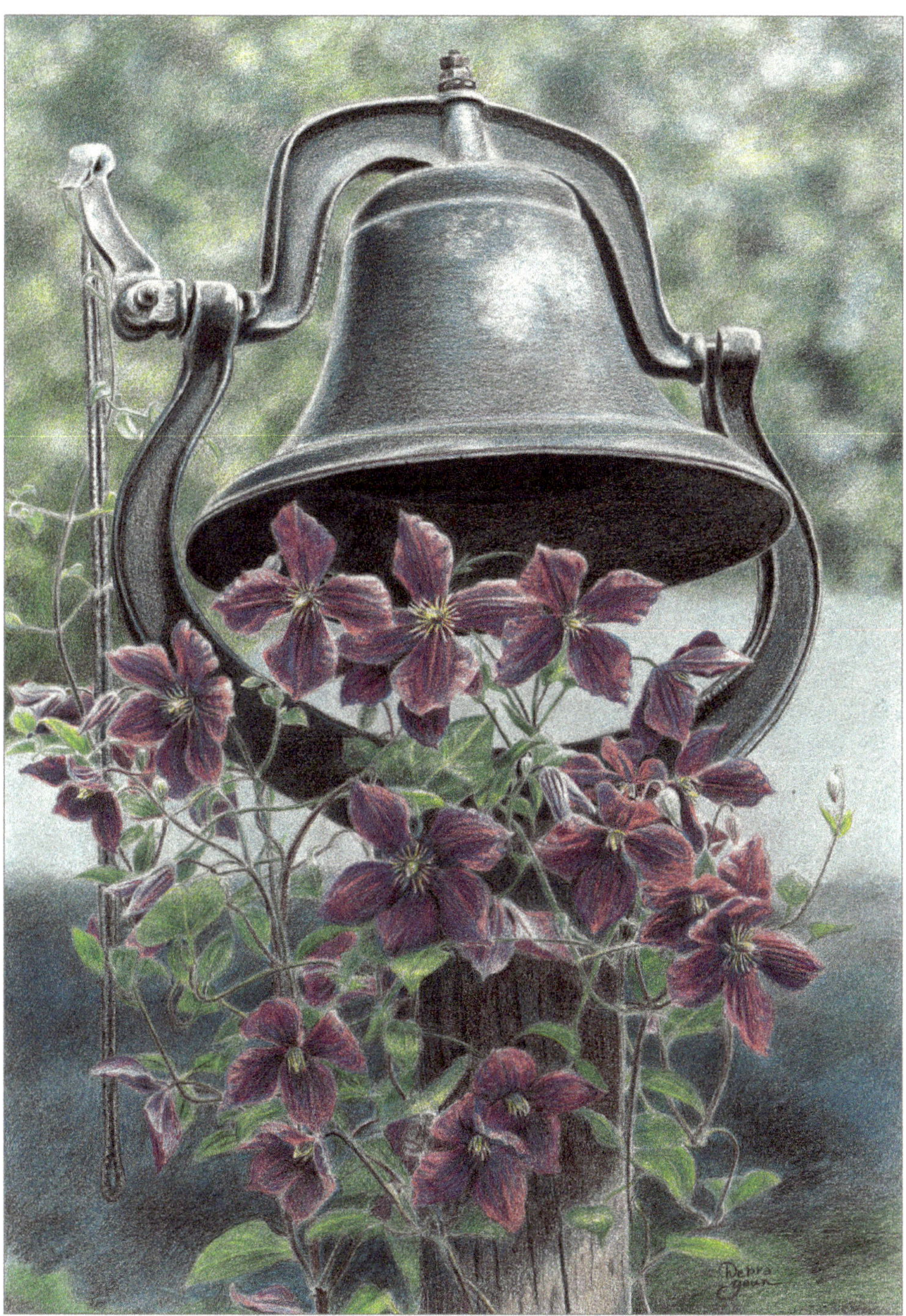

Step Six Next I add canary yellow to some of the leaves, and I darken parts of the background with small circular strokes of cobalt blue. As I add more blue to the magenta flowers, I create a darker purple on the petals. Then I darken some of the leaves with dark green, apply yellow to the center of the flowers, and add more magenta to the petals. I add another layer of black and one of blue to the background, pressing firmly to blend all the layers. I apply a little more black to the bell handle and stand for more contrast. Finally I use white to soften the edges on the petals and buds.

Drawing Animals Accurately

with Debra Yaun

Animals make wonderful subjects to draw because there are so many different kinds to choose from, and they all have their own distinctive features and textures—whether they are smooth and scaled, fluffy and feathered, or soft and furry. In this depiction of "Spike," Debra Yaun uses blending and layering techniques to convey the distinctive patterns in the soft, silky fur of this playful kitten.

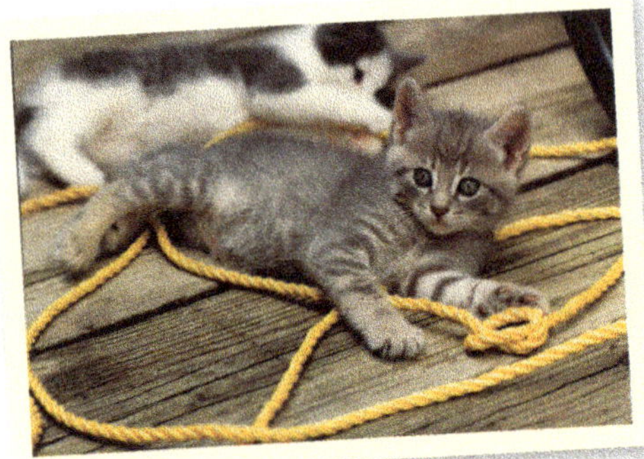

Comparing for Accuracy As I work, I often check my drawing for accuracy by turning it and my reference photo upside down and comparing the two. Looking at them both upside down makes it easier to spot any problems because you're forced to really see the actual object, rather than relying on any preconceptions you may have about what the subject *should* look like.

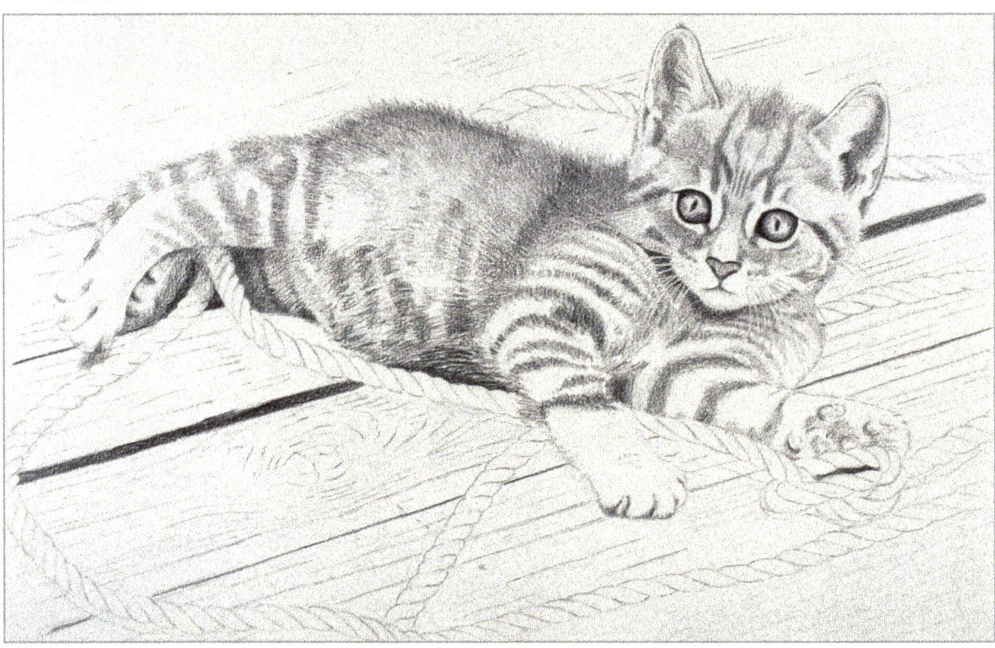

Step One Before I start drawing, I decide to make some slight adjustments from my photo (see "Utilizing Artistic License" on page 60). Then I begin by sketching out the kitten on practice paper, where I make sure I capture Spike's features and proportions accurately. I transfer the drawing to my art paper and erase any excess pencil lines with a kneaded eraser. Next I apply black to the darkest areas around the kitten and lightly layer over the gray areas of the fur. At this point I'm not worried about creating texture; I just apply the various gray values with a fairly sharp pencil, using a circular motion. Then I use gray to fill in around the areas of lighter fur and the area around the whiskers, leaving the whiskers white.

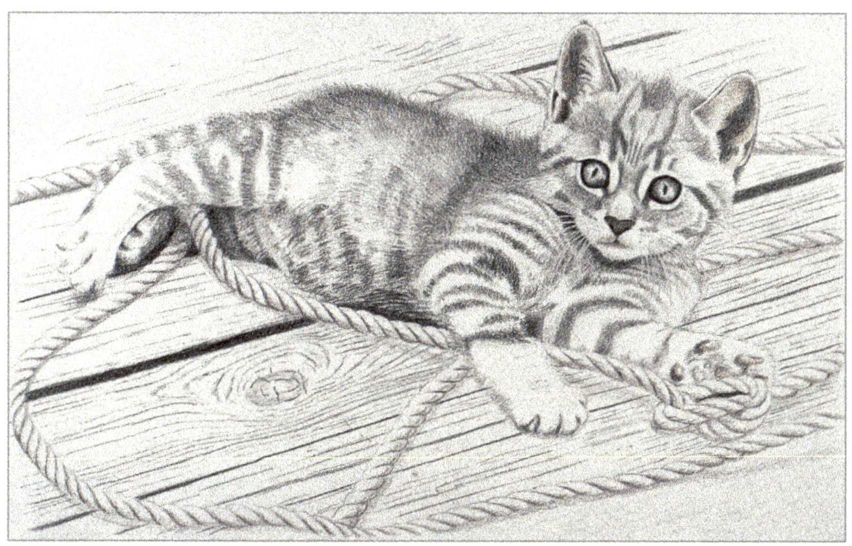

Step Two I apply a light layer of peach to the insides of the ears, to the nose, to the belly, and around the mouth, using circular strokes. I give the upturned paw pads a layer of peach, but I leave the highlights white. I add a light layer of dark umber to the rope and then add a heavier layer on the shadowed side. I also work a light layer of dark umber into the fur and over the paw pads. I detail the wood with black, making sure all the strokes follow the direction of the wood grain.

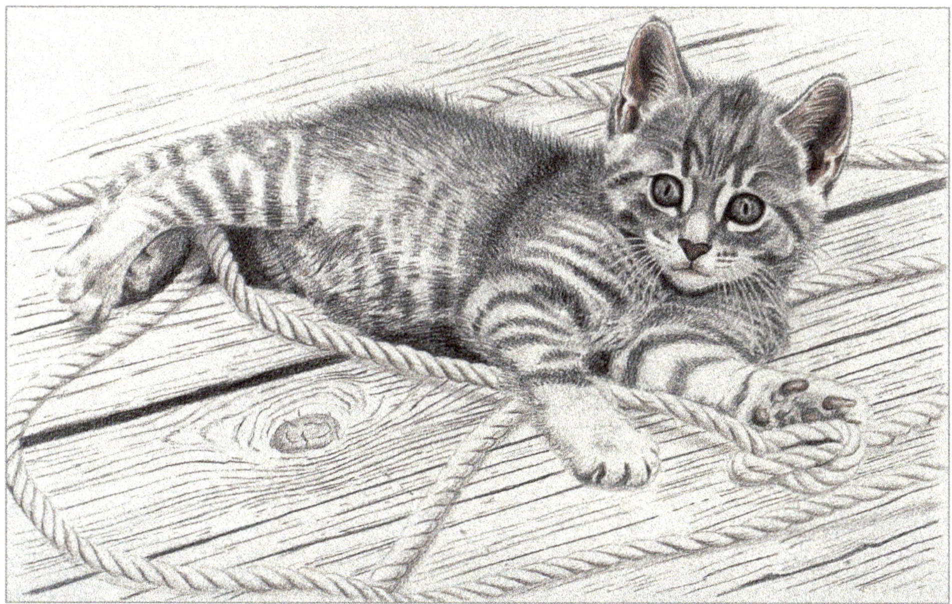

Step Three I lightly apply magenta over the insides of the ears. Then I add light layers of magenta and dark umber to the paw pads, using circular strokes for a soft blend. I soften the black rims around the eyes with dark umber and also add dark umber to the stripes in the fur. I add some more black to the dark grays in the fur and darken some areas of the chest and front legs, using short, tapered strokes that follow the direction the fur grows. Then I add dark umber to the stripes and the darker areas of the hind legs, using a blending stump to soften the colors. I add a ring of dark umber to the eyes around the pupils, and then I use dark umber to draw over the black detail lines in the wood.

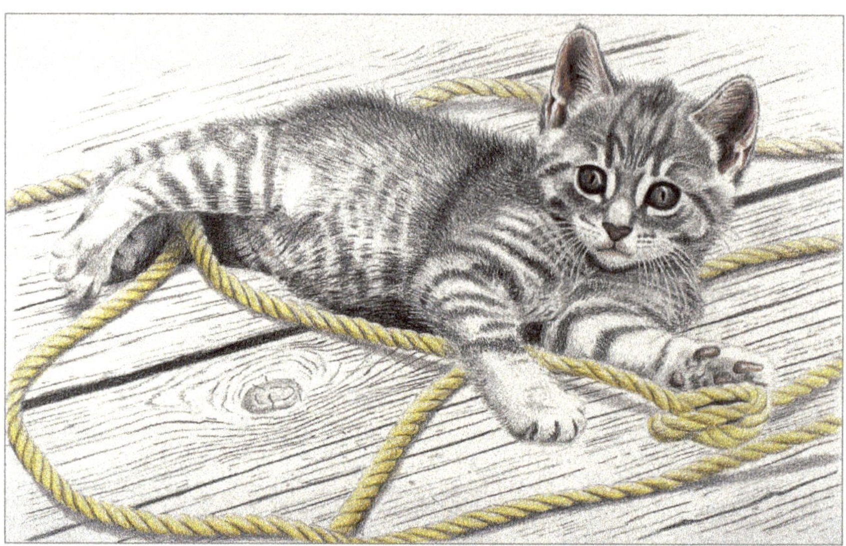

Step Four Next I layer cobalt blue over the irises in the eyes, saving the white highlights. To deepen the shadows, I apply some blue over the chin, under the neck, along the shadow of the front legs, and in all of the shadowed areas of the rope. I also add blue to the back leg and the tail to "push" them back a bit. I add a touch of canary yellow to the eyes between the iris and the pupil. Next I apply yellow to the rope, putting a slightly heavier layer on the strand in the foreground. Then I layer a little black over the rope's blue cast shadow to darken it.

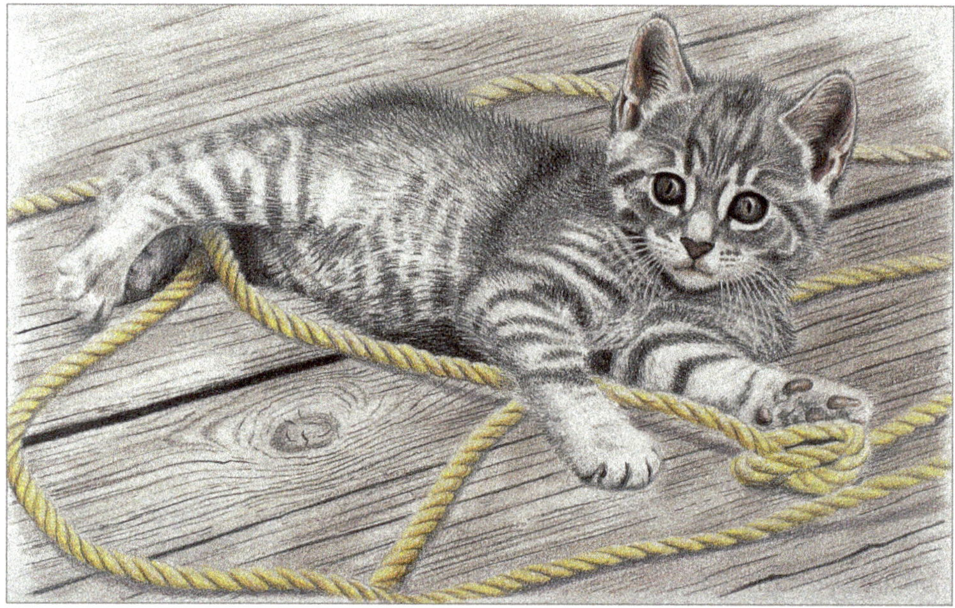

Step Five I apply cobalt blue to the dark cracks of the deck and add a few light strokes of magenta in front of the kitten. Then I add magenta to the shadow under the rope, creating a purple hue. I add a shadow under the knot in the rope and then apply another light layer of dark umber to darken the wood. I lightly add a few spots of canary yellow and use a blending stump to soften the colors. Then I draw the kitten's fur over the wood with black, making short strokes that start at the body and go out in slightly different directions. I refer to my photo here, matching it carefully to render this kitten's particular fur pattern.

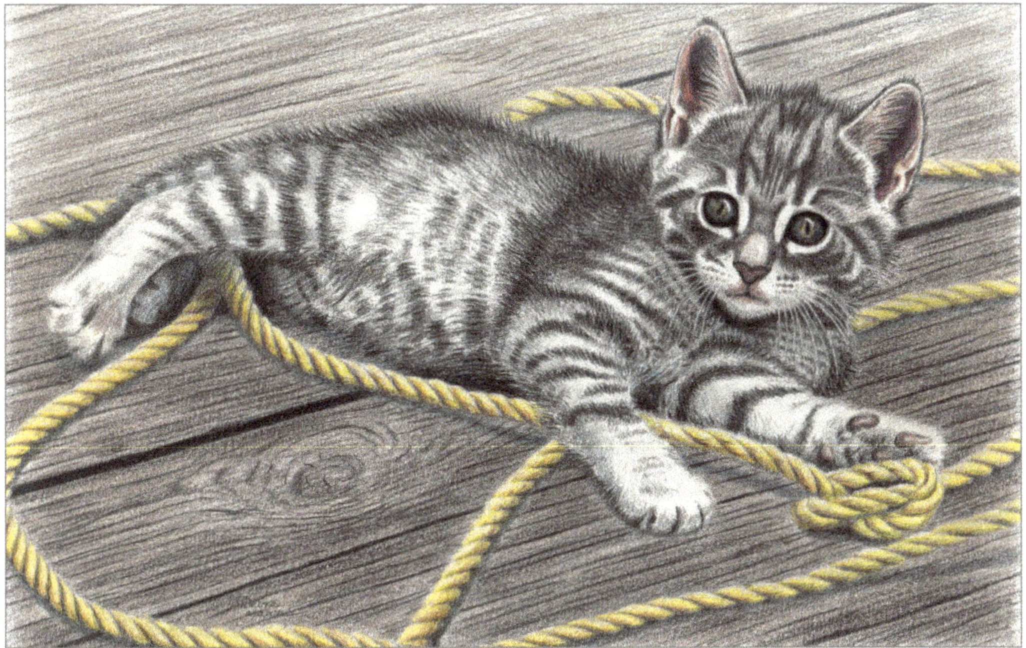

Step Six I soften the fur even more by blending short strokes of white over some of the black. Then I draw white over the whiskers and create a few hard strokes of white through some of the darker areas (such as the belly) to show the texture of the fur. I add a little more cobalt blue, dark umber, and canary yellow to the eyes, then finish with a layer of white to soften and blend the colors. I also add white to the tiny tufts of fur in the ears. The stripes on the legs look a little thin, so I widen them with short black strokes. I darken the shadows under the ropes in a few places with a little more blue and black, but I keep the shadow lighter than it appears in the photo to keep the focus on the kitten. I use white to soften the colors in the rope, and then I turn the drawing upside down again to check the values. I decide to darken the wood a little more, so I add some black and dark umber, mostly in the foreground. Finally I apply a light layer of yellow to warm the color of the wood.

Starting with Black and White

Many colored pencil artists begin with a black-and-white value drawing; this method is called "grisaille." Grisaille allows the artist to establish the darks and lights in a subject before applying color. Then, as the transparent colored pencil values are layered over the initial drawing, the dark values lend additional depth to the darkest areas. The example below demonstrates how the grisaille technique helps build volume in a simple scene.

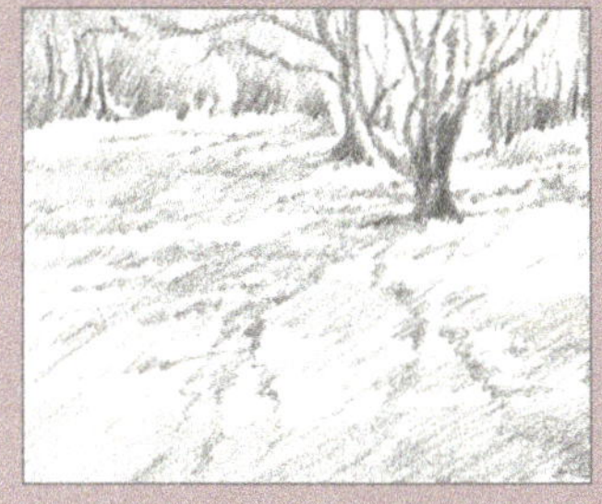

Graphite underdrawing

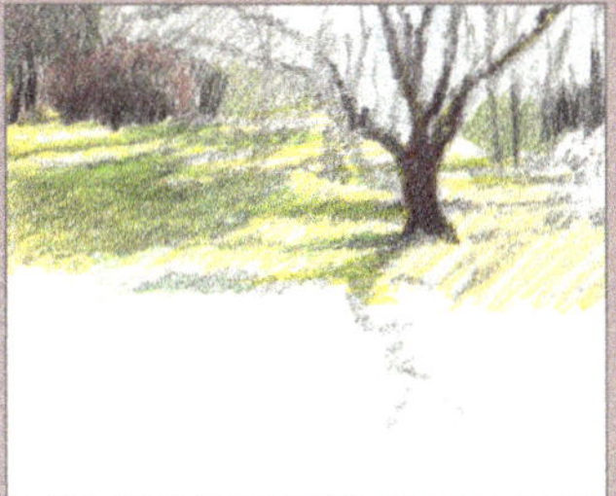

First layer of color

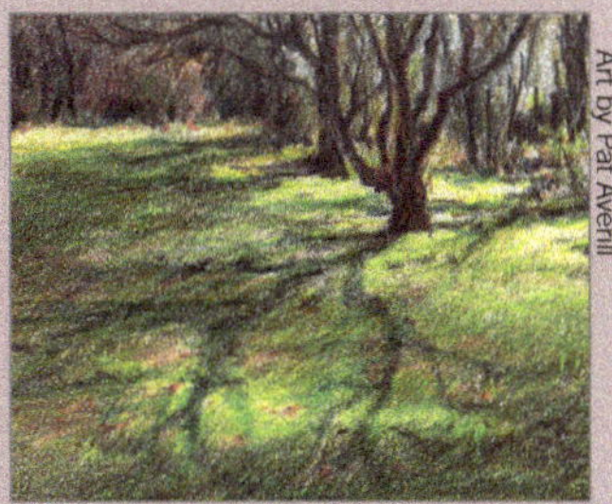

Final drawing

Art by Pat Averill

Achieving a Likeness

with Debra Yaun

Portraits have been extremely popular subjects for centuries; there is nothing quite as exciting as capturing a human personality on paper. You can accurately depict the likeness of a person by carefully observing and copying the shapes, values, and colors you see. Begin by dividing the face into thirds, and note where the features fall in relation to the whole face and to one another (the *proportions*). Then, as you do when drawing animals, look for what makes each person unique. In this portrait of Liza, Debra Yaun communicates the girl's charming innocence by paying close attention to proportion and detail—including her wide smile, wispy curls, and adorable dimples.

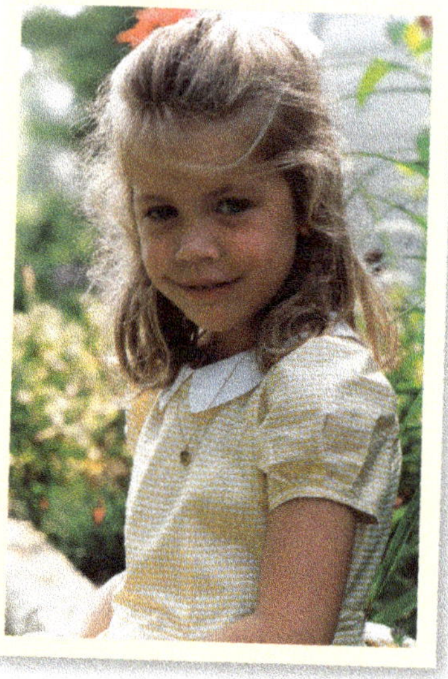

Drawing Children When drawing a portrait, it's important to work out the details and proportions in a sketch before you begin applying color. For example, in this photo reference, you can see that the halfway mark between the top of the head and the chin is just about at eye level. When the sketch is complete, I transfer the drawing of Liza to my art paper.

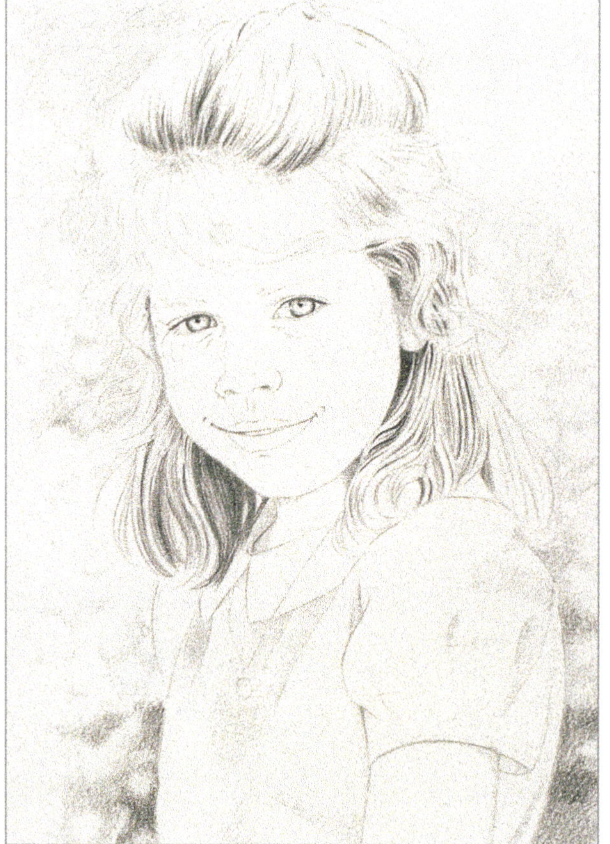

Step One Using light, short strokes of black, I begin by placing some shadows on the dress. I create a loose indication of flowers in the background and a dark, leafy area near the bottom. Next I apply black in a circular motion to smooth out the background, drawing around the lighter areas. Then I indicate the shadows in the hair with soft black lines that follow the direction the hair curls.

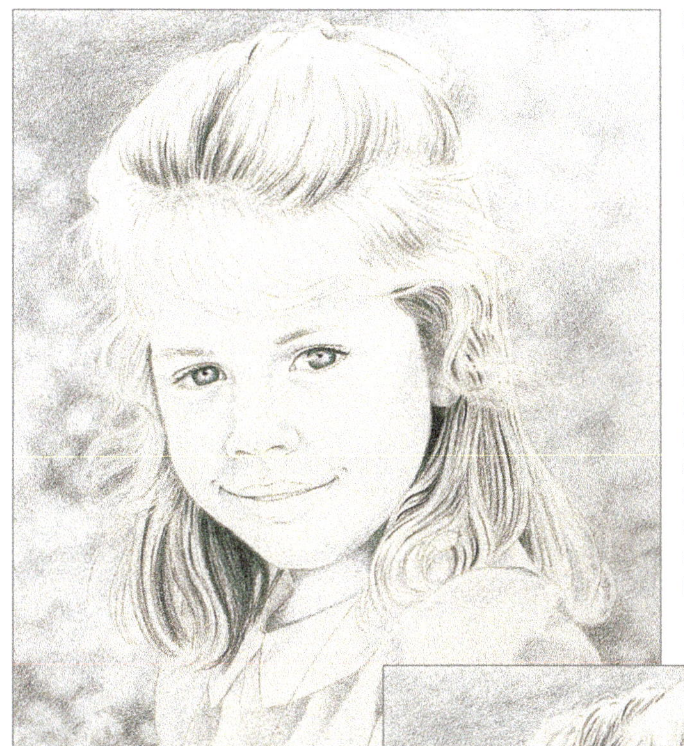

Step Two I lightly indicate the eyebrows with black, stroking in the direction they grow. I lightly apply cobalt blue to the shadows on the face and arm, and then I layer blue over the black lines in the hair to soften them and make them less stark. I also add a little blue to the white of the eyes and under the eyelashes to give the eyes some dimension. Then I apply blue over the shadows on the dress and add a little more black in the background. I give most of the background a light layer of blue, pressing harder over the black areas that I want to appear a bit darker. I leave the wisps of hair along the sides of the face white by coloring around them with the background colors. Then I use a blending stump to blend the blue into the background.

Step Three I layer dark umber over the black lines in the hair, pressing firmly in the dark areas. Then I lightly apply dark umber to the rest of the hair, leaving the highlights white. I softly add dark umber to the crease of the eyelids, the corners of the mouth, and the dimples that make her expression so unique. I also apply a light layer of dark umber to the lips, leaving the highlight on the bottom lip white. Next I detail the eyelashes with dark umber, starting at the lid and curving them out. Then I make the eyebrows a little darker with black.

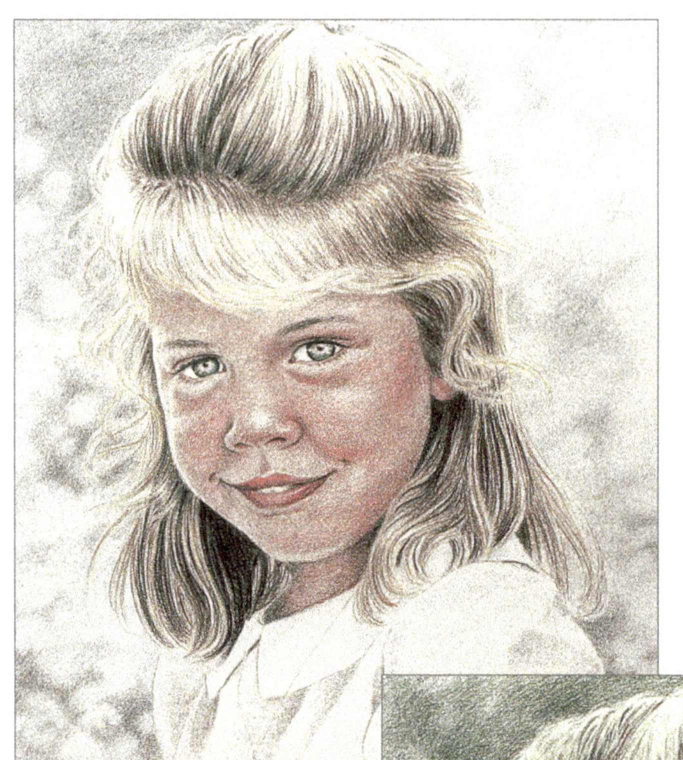

Step Four To establish a base for the skin tones, I add a light, smooth layer of magenta to the face and arm, leaving the highlighted edge of the cheek white. Then I use a blending stump on the skin tones to lightly blend the colors. Where the face appears too red, I pull some pigment off with a kneaded eraser. I apply a little magenta to the inner corner of each eye, and then I add a light layer of canary yellow over the hair and face. I darken the hair with a little more dark umber and lightly indicate a few freckles on the nose and cheeks.

Step Five Next I apply a light layer of peach in the whites of the eyes, leaving a small white highlight in the center of each pupil. I also add a light layer of peach to the teeth (since they are in shadow and shouldn't be pure white) and most of the face, leaving highlights on the nose and bottom lip. Next I softly apply peach to the highlighted edge of the cheek, smoothing the transition from color to white. In the background, I add areas of dark umber, dark green, and black to the smooth, circular shapes. Then I apply green over the black in the top-left and bottom-right corners. I add a little more brown to the arm and sleeve to create a sense of depth and realism.

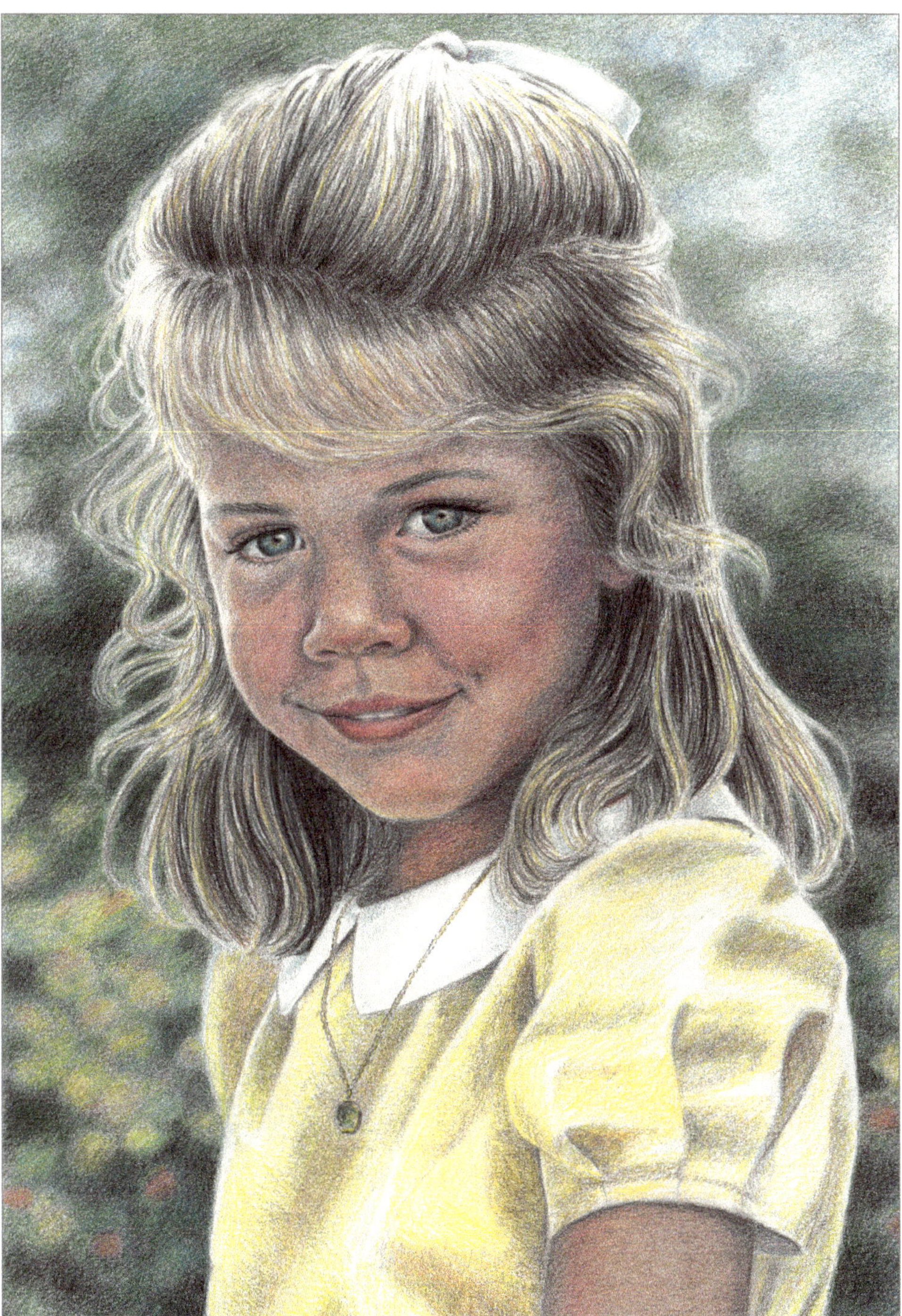

Step Six I add magenta to the hair and then layer white over the darks. I use dark umber to draw the necklace and locket, then add canary yellow. I apply dark green and magenta to the background, then use cobalt blue to soften the colors. I lightly layer magenta and then dark umber over the blue shadows on the dress and blend with a stump. Then I apply canary yellow over the dress, leaving highlights as needed. I lightly layer blue along the right side of the face, along the hairline and cheek, to round out the face. Finally I soften some of the wisps of hair and darken the eyelashes and eyebrows.

Composing a Landscape

with Pat Averill

Nature produces amazingly beautiful scenes that call out to be captured on paper. But a good landscape drawing has more than just an interesting subject—it also has a dynamic composition. *Composition* refers to the relationships among the objects in a scene, and a good composition uses interesting colors, shapes, and lines to lead the viewer's eye in and around the drawing, toward the *center of interest* (also referred to as the "focal point"). In this rendering of a nature preserve, Pat Averill uses a few simple guidelines (such as the careful placement of the center of interest and the horizon line) to create her composition and draw a compelling outdoor scene.

The Rule of Thirds

It's rarely a good idea to place your center of interest squarely in the middle of the paper. The result is a static composition, with nowhere for the eye to go. To place the center of interest, use the *rule of thirds*—a guideline artists use to divide the picture area into thirds, horizontally and vertically. Fold a piece of paper in thirds in both directions, as shown at right. This creates a grid of nine small rectangles; any of the four corners of the middle rectangle (marked with orange circles in this example) will make a good place for the center of interest.

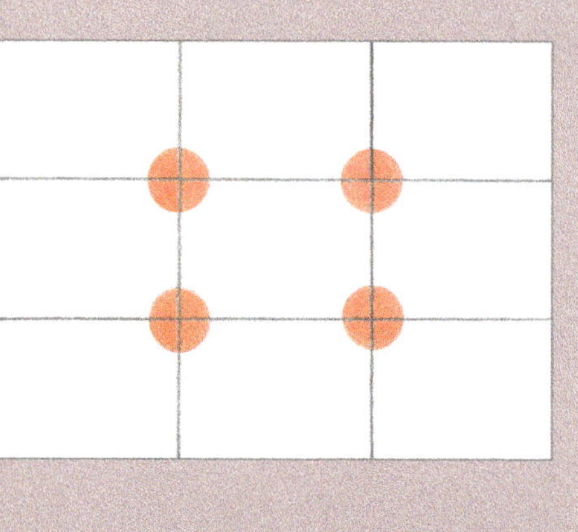

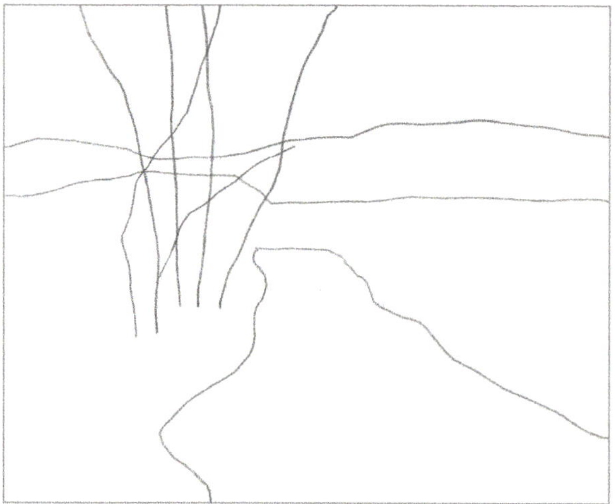

Step One On white, *hot-press* (smooth textured) watercolor paper, I draw a light 8" x 10" border and divide the area into thirds. Then I put drafting tape outside of the pencil lines to keep the paper edges clean. I use the rule of thirds to place my center of interest: the stand of trees in the upper left. I draw six simple lines for the trees, using light pressure and a semi-dull pencil. Then I draw the *horizon line*, another line above for the distant trees, and two lines outlining the stream.

Scraping Out Color

You don't have to impress a line into the paper to get highlights —you can also remove small areas of color by scraping pigment away (called "sgraffito"). Sgraffito is considered a "negative" drawing technique, because you create form and texture by removing color instead of applying it. You can use a craft knife, a razor blade, scissors, or a straight pin to scrape out varying amounts of color, but remember that sgraffito works best on heavy layers of color (so the paper is not damaged).

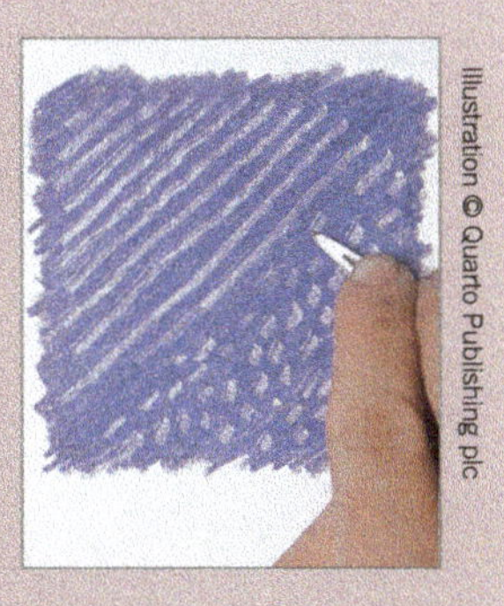

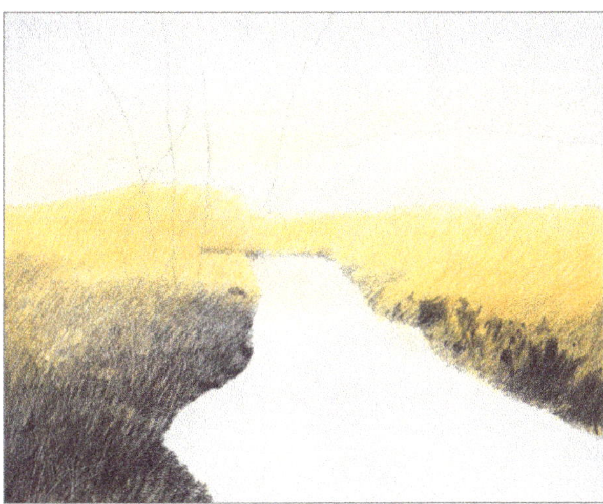

Step Two To create a sense of atmosphere, I apply ivory at the horizon line with hatch strokes. Then I layer light flesh over the lower half of the sky and into the top of the water. I add light violet over the rest of the sky and the water, softly blending the edges. To mark where I will "save" white for the light grasses in the foreground, I use the nib of a stylus to impress wispy, vertical lines in the paper. Next I apply ochre in the grasses with short hatch strokes. I darken the water edges and apply black grape in the same manner over the grass, gradually lessening the pressure as I go up the page to lighten the value and create the illusion of depth. Then I use a sharp ivory pencil to lighten the top edge of the yellow grass.

Step Three I use olive green and light hatch strokes to fill in the distant hills. With light pressure, I darken the top edges of the sky using light blue and short, vertical strokes. At the lower water edge, I make heavy vertical strokes with the same color, gradually lessening the pressure as I go up the page. Using a semi-dull olive green pencil, I layer over the left foreground grass with a combination of hatch and vertical strokes that simulate the way grass grows. On the right side of the water, I apply olive green with a sharp pencil to create the grass in front of the trees and along the water's edge. For the tall trees in the background, I use olive green with light pressure and vertical strokes.

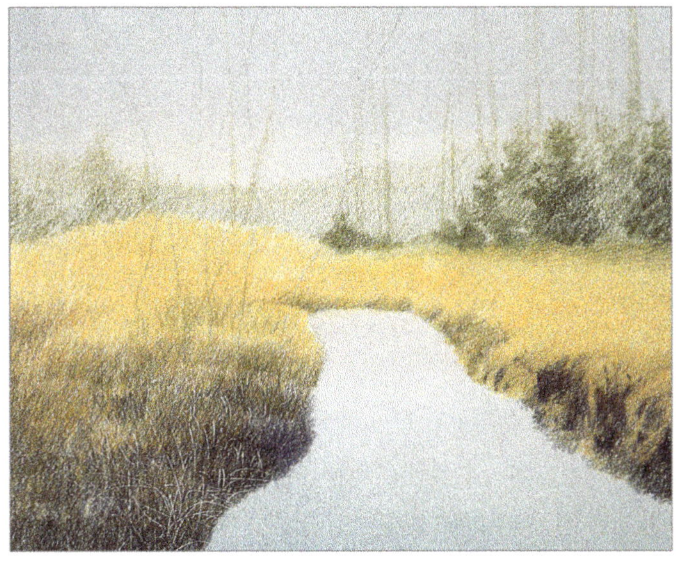

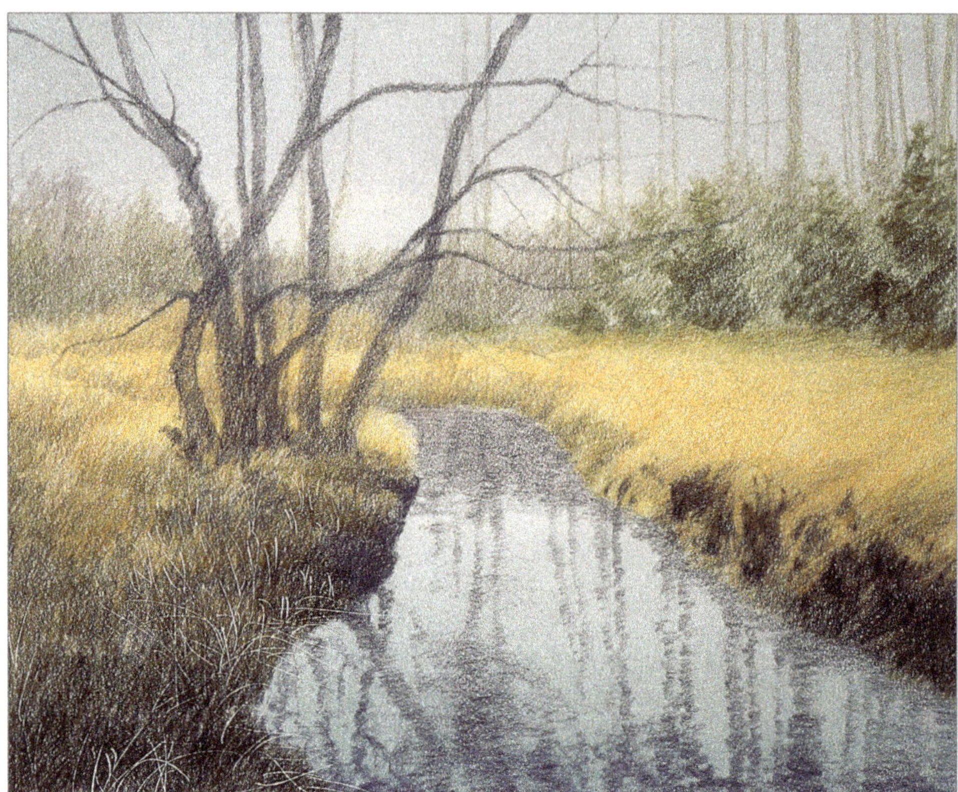

Step Four Using a sharp black grape pencil, I outline the edges of the dark distant trees and fill them in with hatch strokes and medium pressure. Then I add some branches following the original direction of the tree line. Again using medium pressure, I block in the water reflections with black grape and move down the page in a vertical path using short, horizontal strokes. (I use a transparent ruler to make sure the reflections mirror the angles of the trees.) On the land under the big trees, I layer additional black grape with heavier pressure to obtain darker values. I use a sharp clay rose pencil and medium pressure to go over the olive green in the background trees and to go over the tall trees in the background. I also use clay rose to darken the horizontal edge of the stream and to create a flat base under the yellow grassy hill.

Color and Shadow

Before adding color to a drawing, determine the direction and the strength of the light source. Shadows take on different colors depending on the time of day and direction of light. For example, a green tree in bright sun appears to have yellow leaves, a shade of purple or red for the trunk, and a purple-gray cast shadow. In lower light (at sunset), the same tree would look much darker and would have orange highlights; its trunk would be a shade of red-orange, and it would cast a blue shadow.

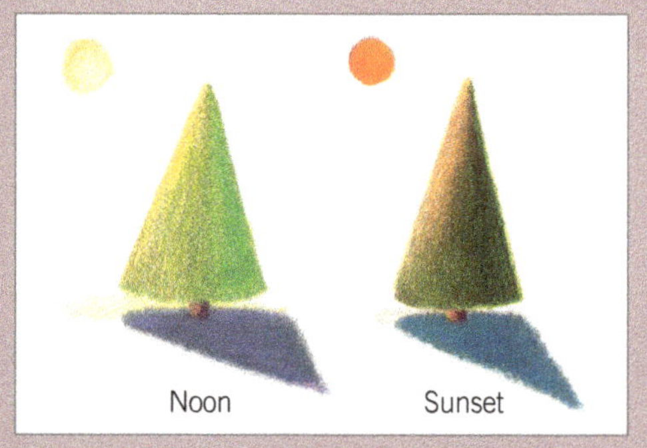

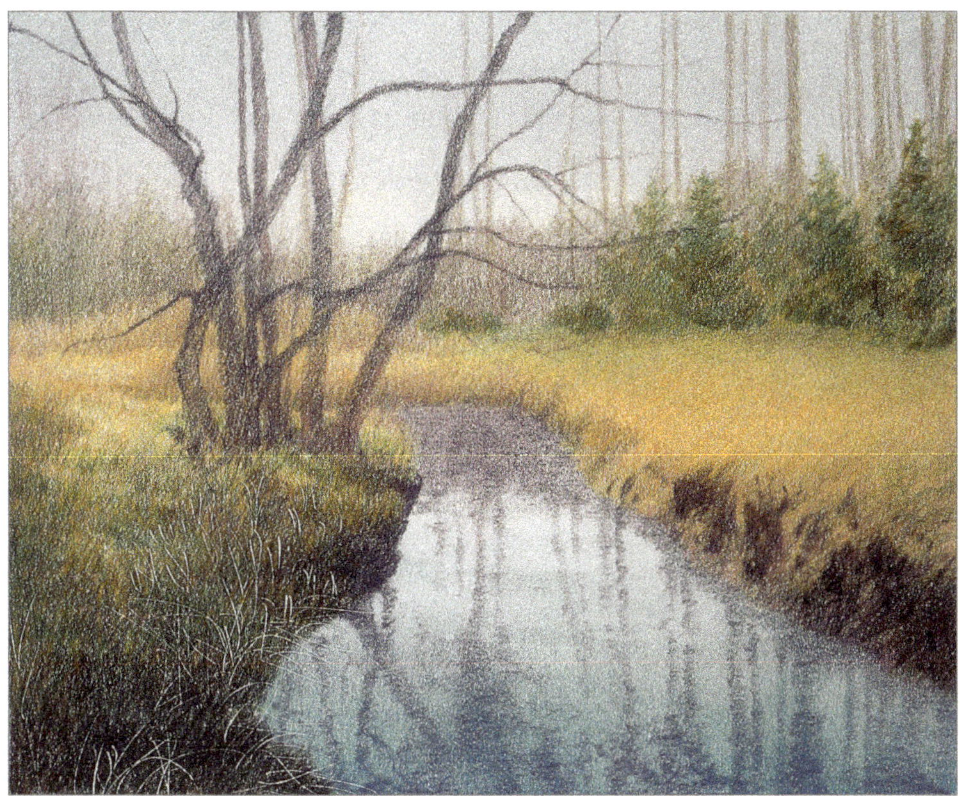

Step Five To create atmosphere, I sharpen a dark flesh pencil and layer over the trees, hills, grasses, and water reflections with light to medium pressure and vertical strokes. I apply ochre and then dark green in the trees above the grass with a sharp pencil and vertical strokes, varying pressure to give dimension to the trees. Under the big trees on the left, I use a sharp dark green pencil with medium to heavy pressure to make short, vertical strokes for the grass. I lift out some color with reusable tack (see page 46) to make a path to the left of the big trees—I knead the tack, pinch it into the shape I want, and then lift out color. On the right side, I lightly scribble dark green on the lower half of the grass. Under the trees on the right, I use a nearly horizontal stroke to lightly layer dark green on the grass.

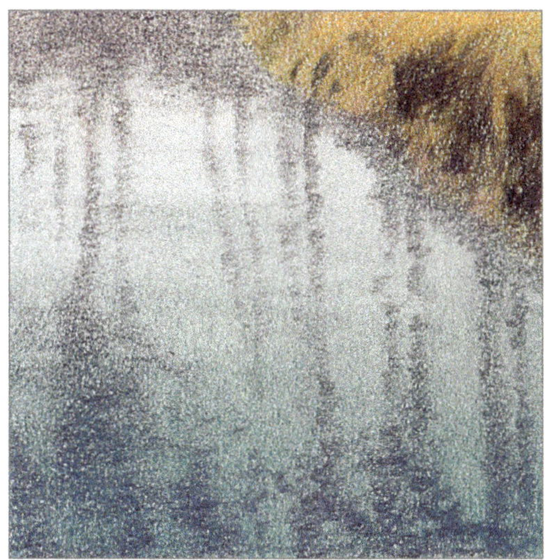

Reflection Detail To add depth to the water in the lower foreground, I add a layer of true blue with vertical strokes, gradually adjusting from heavy to light pressure as I work toward the bottom of the paper.

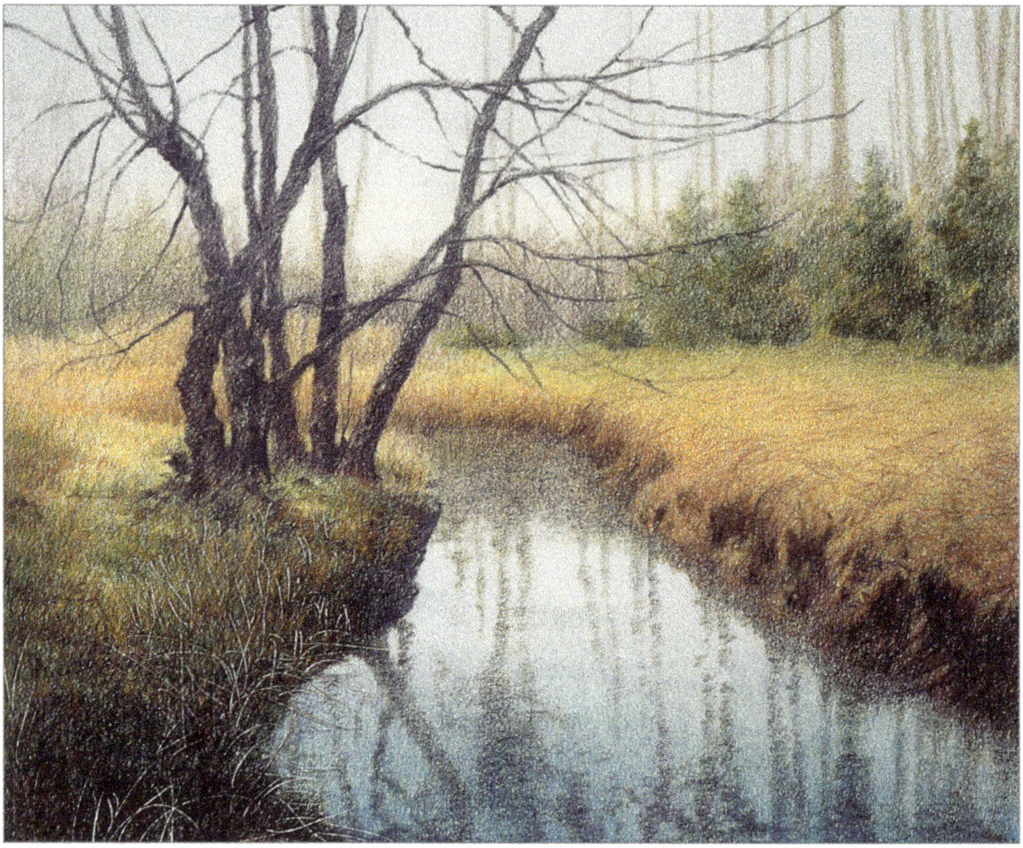

Step Six I adjust the tree reflections in the water with a sharp olive green pencil, light pressure, and vertical strokes. For the big trees, I apply a medium to heavy layer of black grape, outlining first and then filling in with short hatch strokes. For the foreground grasses on each side of the water, I scribble with a sharp black grape pencil to add texture. I also use black grape to darken the shadows in the stream bank, to deepen the base of the big trees and the distant hills, and to glaze over the green trees above the yellow grass. I use a sharp terra cotta pencil with medium pressure to make some short, vertical strokes on the left side in the grass and above the bend in the water, and then I scribble the same color along the right bank.

Tree Trunk Detail I lift out some color in the tree trunks with reusable tack to create more texture (see page 46). At this point, I decide to add a few more limbs on the trees, using a sharp black grape pencil and lessening the pressure occasionally to give the impression of light over a round limb.

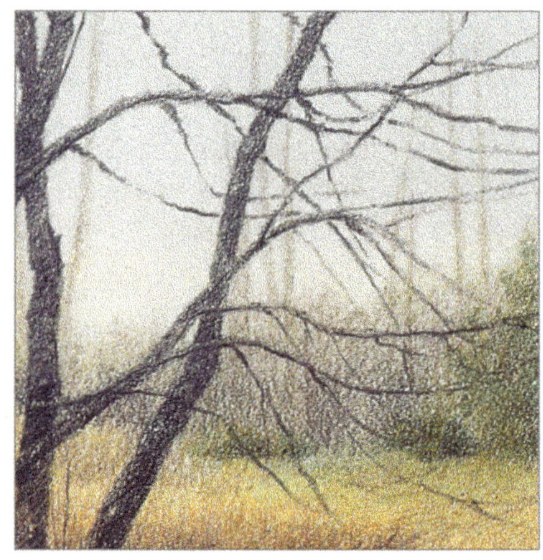

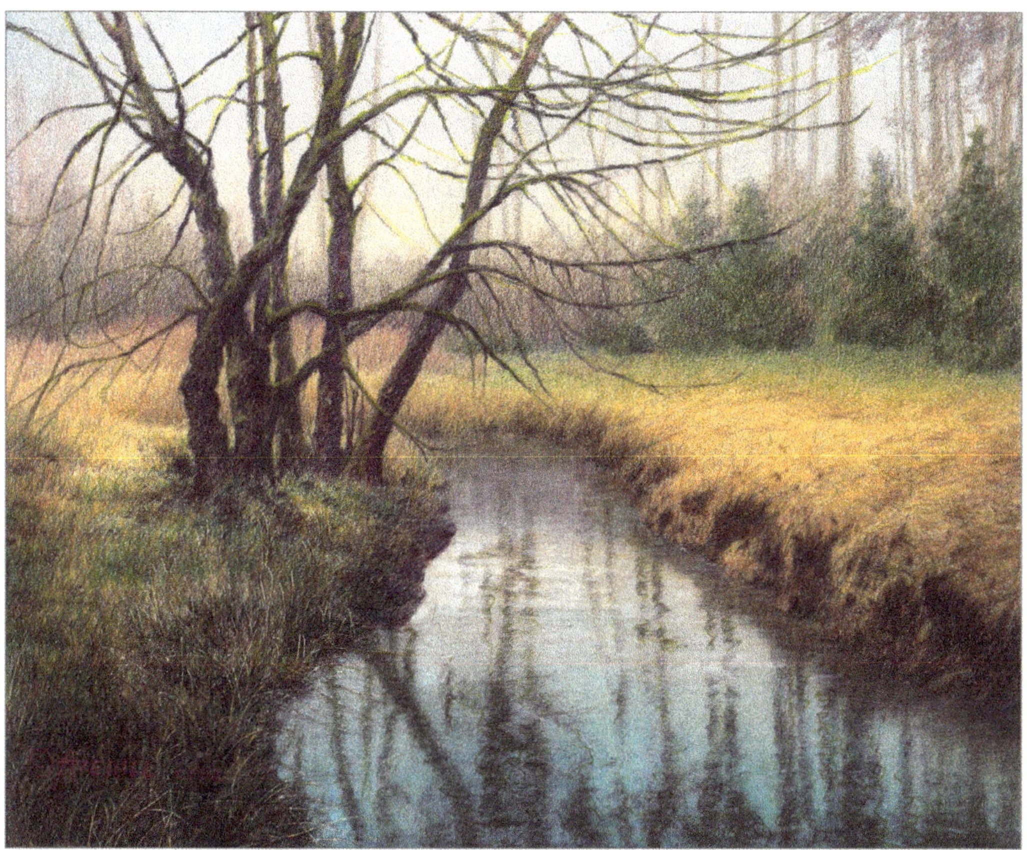

Step Seven With a sharp black grape pencil, heavy pressure, and a linear stroke, I add more limbs and dark spots in the main trees, and I make hard edges where the water and land meet on the left. Where moss covers the tree limbs, I apply chartreuse with medium pressure and a stroke that follows the direction of the limbs. Next I use a sharp ochre pencil with heavy pressure and a scribble stroke to go over the grass, leaving some areas of green grass and shadow areas to show through. With clay rose, I make a few sweeping suggestions of tree limbs in the upper-right stand of trees, using medium pressure and hatch strokes. To create more warmth in the grass near the water, I apply Tuscan red with varying pressure and scribble strokes. Next I use indigo blue to lightly correct the overly red tone in the darkest shadows, especially on the right bank. In the distant clump of grass, I apply light carmine with vertical strokes and light pressure. To make the water look glassy, I use a blending pencil, first with heavy pressure and vertical strokes and then with light pressure and horizontal strokes. Finally I add a few horizontal strokes of a dull white pencil next to the distant water's edge. Wherever needed, I add more of the same colors over the blending pencil to revive their brilliance.

Capturing Mood

with Pat Averill

Many times the most captivating characteristic about a subject is the feeling it evokes in the viewer. For example, the energy of a bustling street scene or the serenity of a peaceful meadow can be captivating. So how do you translate the mood of a scene to paper? With color! In general, warm colors portray a sunny, upbeat mood, whereas cool colors seem more calm or mysterious. For example, a sunlit field of bright yellow flowers seems cheerful and invigorating, whereas a quiet harbor blanketed in blue-gray fog appears serene and still. In this drawing, Pat Averill uses layers of dark, muted hues to capture the tranquil feeling of a deserted beach at dusk.

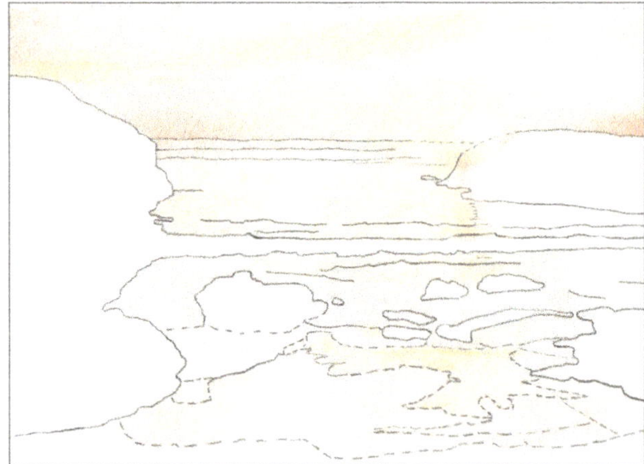

Step One I make a simple line drawing using dashes where I see soft edges. I erase any pencil marks around the setting sun and use a sharp ivory pencil with crosshatch strokes and heavy pressure to color the brightest areas around it. In the area where the water meets the sand, I apply another layer of ivory with heavier pressure. Around the ivory color in the sky, I add light flesh, using the same strokes and medium pressure. On the left and right sides of the horizon line, I apply a second layer of light flesh. Then I layer vertical strokes of light flesh over the water and wet sand, using a sharp pencil and medium pressure.

Step Two Over the rocks and in the darkest areas of the water and sand, I apply several layers of black grape using medium-heavy pressure and hatch strokes. Next I vary the widths of the waves as I continue to layer on black grape with hatch strokes and medium-heavy pressure. I check my photo frequently to make sure I draw the angles in the waves correctly.

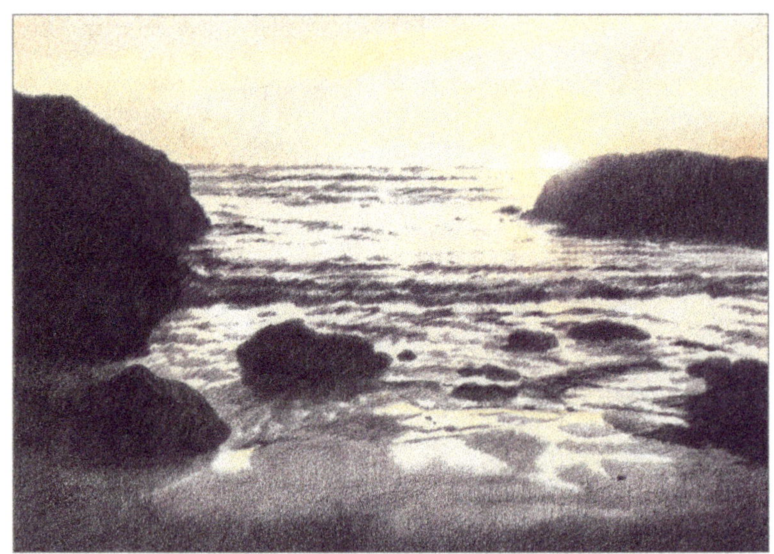

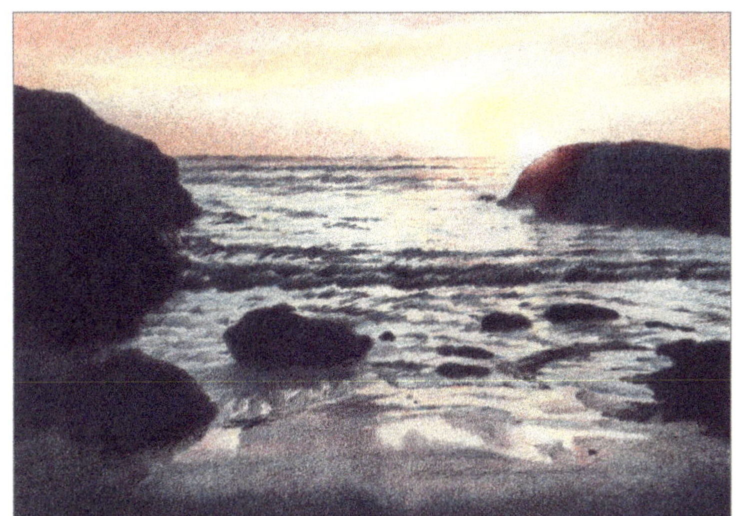

Step Three I outline the tops of the rocks with indigo blue, and then I use the same color and crosshatch strokes to fill in the rocks and the darkest sand. Still using indigo blue, I darken the shadows of the waves and the distant water. I apply rose carmine at the horizon and just below, leaving white paper for a bright reflection. Using rose car mine, I color over the headland, easing the pressure as I work closer to the sun. To darken the clouds and fog, I add several layers with hatch strokes.

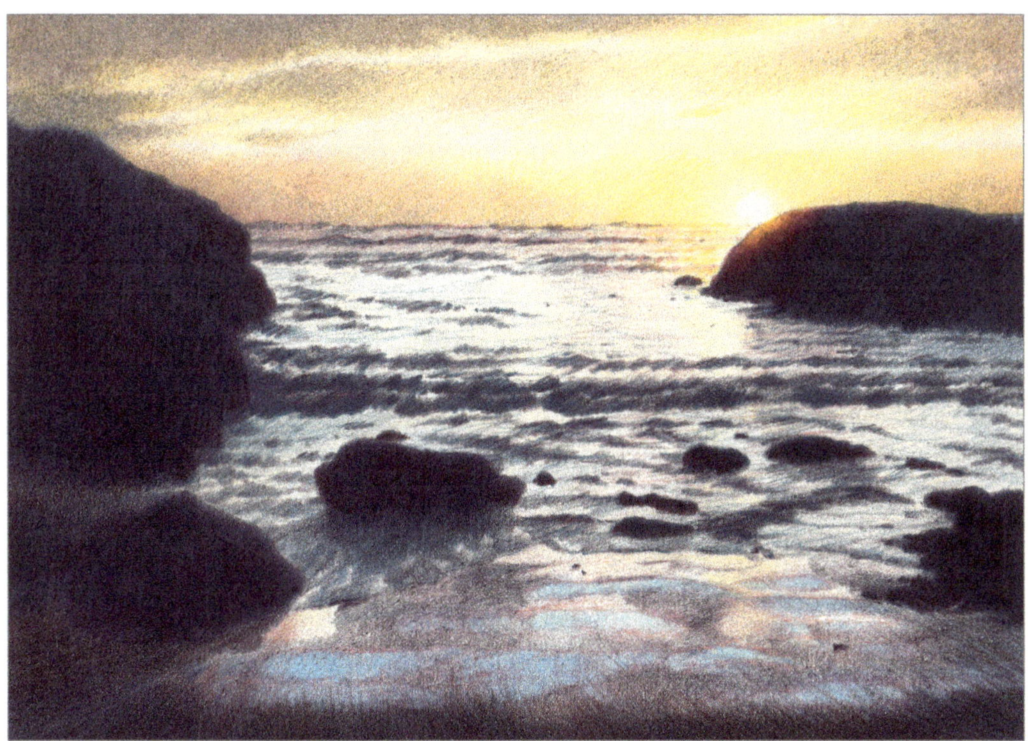

Step Four I darken the clouds with 30% warm gray, and then I use light blue and rose carmine to create the reflections in the wet sand. I add Tuscan red with crosshatch strokes over the dark rocks and darkest sand. Then I add crosshatches of canary yellow and rose carmine to the edge of the rock directly under the setting sun. Next I use hatch strokes of canary yellow around the sun and in the clouds. In the water below the sun, I add a few horizontal waves with the same color.

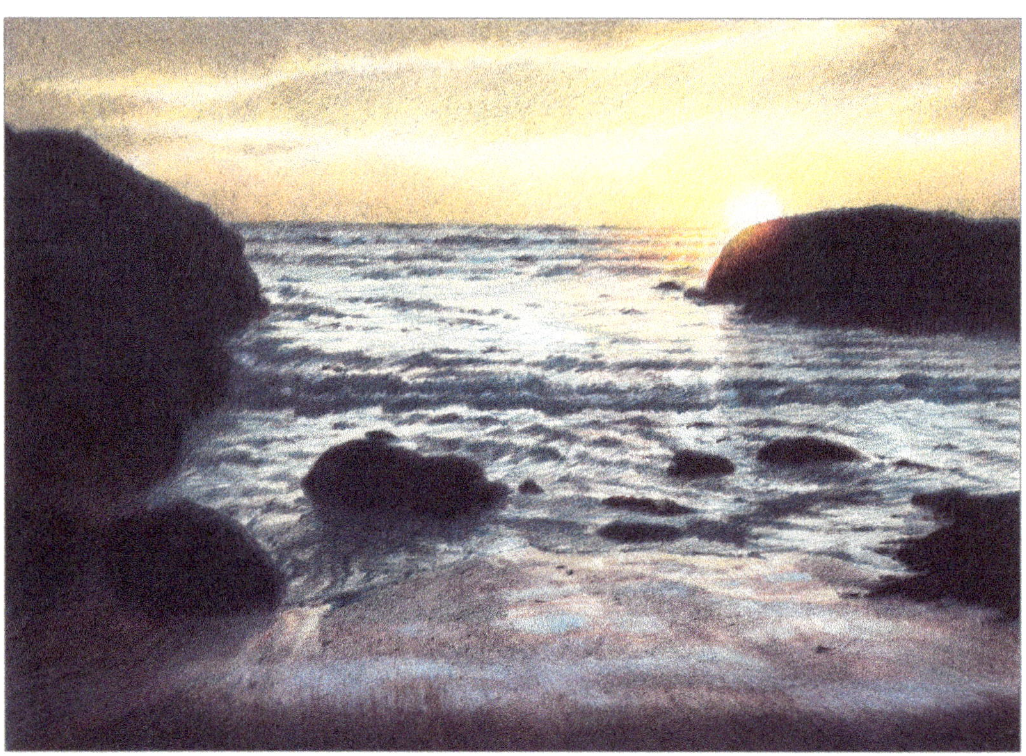

Step Five I lift out color with reusable tack (see below) where I want sky reflections on the white foam, and then I use a sharp light blue pencil and diagonal strokes to fill in the breaking waves. I start to develop shadows in the water patterns with black grape and indigo blue, using medium to heavy pressure. Accurately rendering light and shadow is more important than getting each wave to match the photo, so I check my progress in dim light; groupings of dark and light values are easier to see this way. I blend the dark foreground sand with a blending pencil, using heavy pressure and following the same direction as the strokes of color in the sand.

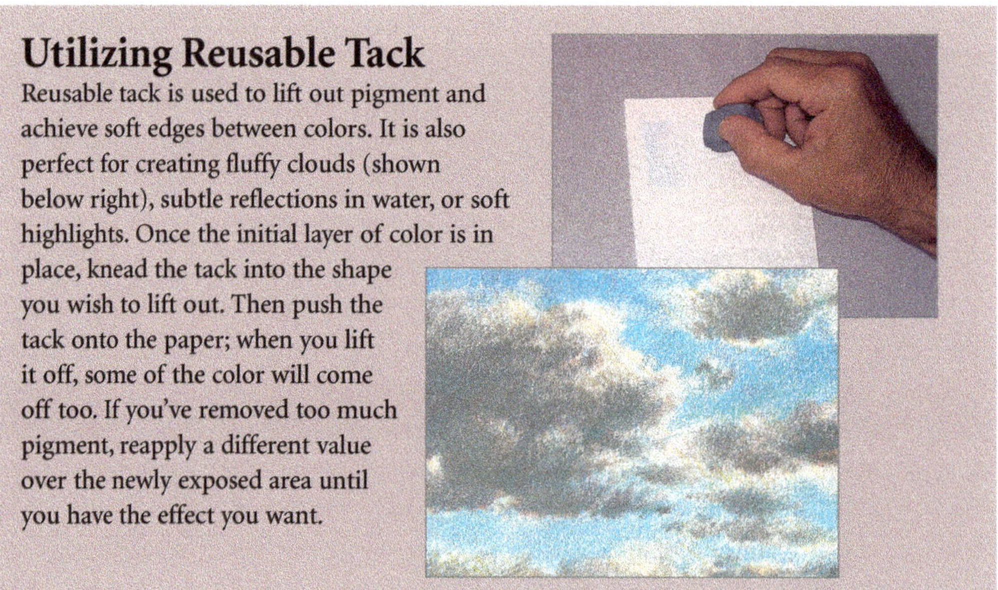

Utilizing Reusable Tack

Reusable tack is used to lift out pigment and achieve soft edges between colors. It is also perfect for creating fluffy clouds (shown below right), subtle reflections in water, or soft highlights. Once the initial layer of color is in place, knead the tack into the shape you wish to lift out. Then push the tack onto the paper; when you lift it off, some of the color will come off too. If you've removed too much pigment, reapply a different value over the newly exposed area until you have the effect you want.

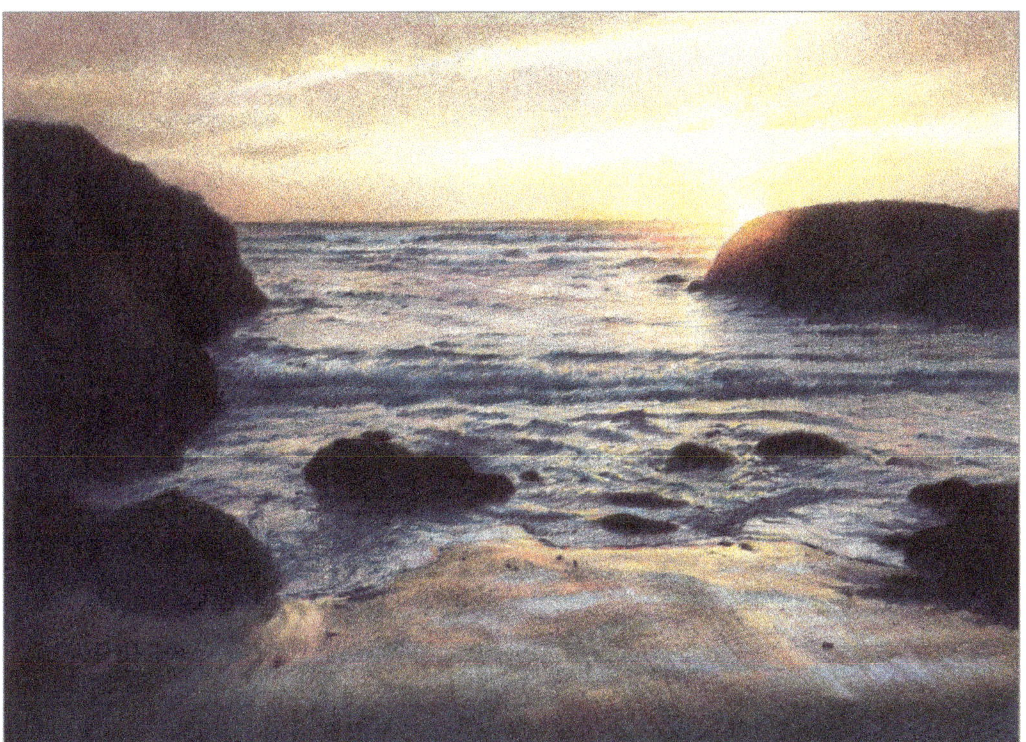

Step Six Wherever I want more color in the clouds and fog, I use a sharp clay rose pencil with medium to light pressure to apply hatch strokes. Using crosshatch strokes and medium pressure, I apply canary yellow to the sunset reflections on the wet sand. Then I add a light glaze of canary yellow followed by dark flesh over the dark areas of the sand, leaving the blue reflections untouched. In the water directly under the sun, I draw the wave patterns with canary yellow. Then I glaze the water with dark flesh, using vertical strokes and medium pressure. To suggest shapes on the dark rocks, I lightly glaze over them with canary yellow, using crosshatch strokes. I pull the shadow areas together in the ocean by using a sharp indigo blue pencil with light pressure and loose, almost horizontal strokes. Finally I use canary yellow to glaze over the darkest sand in the foreground.

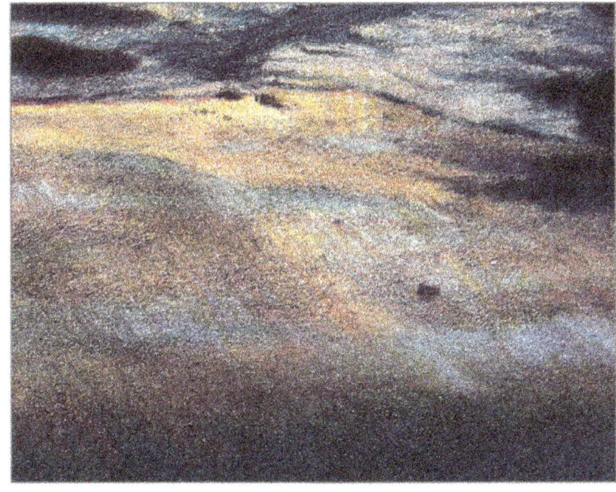

Wet Sand Detail To give a better sense of depth and perspective to the scene, I use a dull black grape pencil to create a pattern in the wet sand that radiates out from the water, making it seem as if the waves have just rushed back into the ocean.

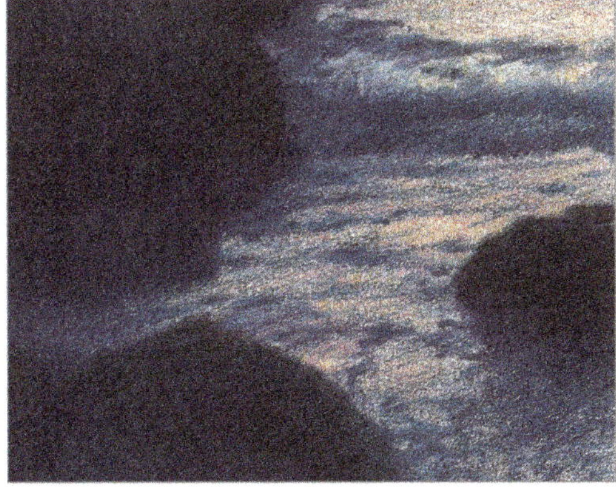

Rocks and Water Detail Whenever you add more dark values to a scene, the light values seem to fade away. But color correction is easy; here I just add another layer of indigo blue to the dark values in the rocks and water to cool the Tuscan red I applied in step four.

Understanding Value

with Pat Averill

Artistic expression is rewarding, regardless of whether your art is representational or stylized. In either case, you will need to learn to see the different values in your subjects because it is the variation among the light and dark values that creates the illusion of three-dimensional form in your drawings. Drawing the outline defines the object's shape, but adding the varying values gives a sense of form. Try squinting when you look at your subject to see the values more clearly; squinting helps eliminate the details and simplify the shapes. In Pat Averill's depiction of a charming rural scene, you can see how the contrasts between the lights and darks gives both form and dimension to the trees and makes the water wheel appear cylindrical and three-dimensional.

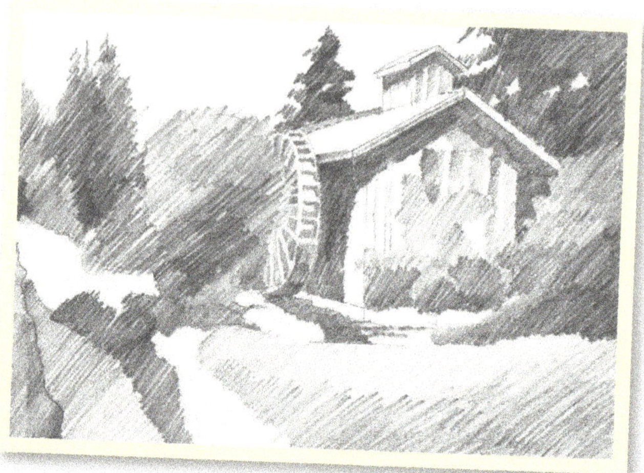

Using Value Studies Creating a value study of your subject can help you identify where to place the lightest and darkest colors in your drawing. In this case, I began with a photocopy of my original color photo to reduce the scene to black and white. The photocopy also obscured some of the details, so I was better able to carefully observe the values in the scene. I found that the lightest values are in the sky, the medium values are in the grass and the flowers, and the darkest values are in the trees and the building. I also sketched in the large masses in the scene to help guide my placement of color later.

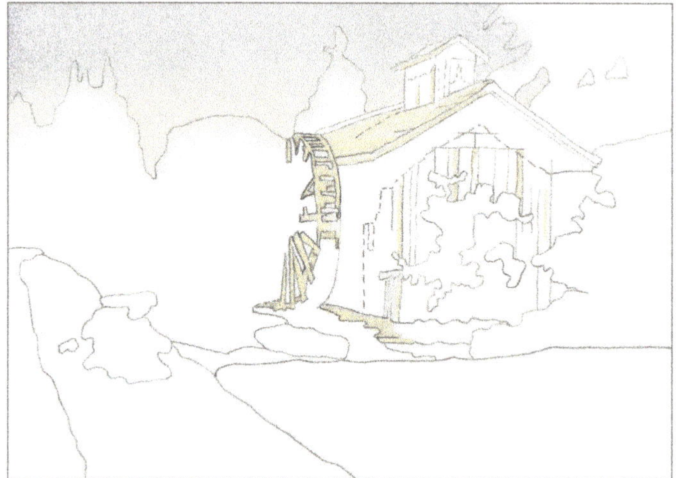

Step One I tape a copy of the photo to a window, tape lightweight copy paper over it, and use a graphite pencil to trace the outlines of the general shapes. I transfer the lines to my art paper and add color, using quick, vertical strokes and a light flesh pencil to fill in the lower sky. Then I add a layer of light violet, overlapping the flesh color a bit. Where I see the light values in the water wheel and in other bright areas, I use a blending pencil with heavy pressure to outline and fill in the shapes; this will cause the subsequent layers of color to appear lighter.

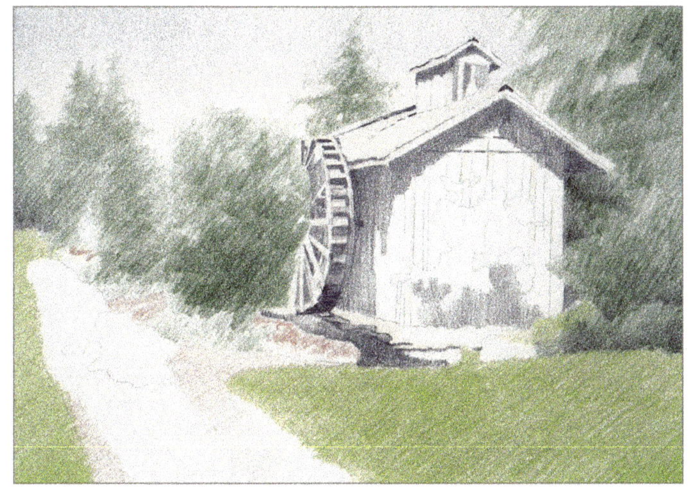

Step Two I use black grape to create shadows in and around the water wheel and the mill, drawing outlines first and then filling them in using medium to heavy pressure. I also add black grape to the base of the distant trees to create shadows above the grass. Next I use a semi-sharp dark green pencil to fill in the background trees with hatch strokes. Then I fill in the grass with a semi-sharp moss green pencil, medium pressure, and hatch strokes. I color the pink flowers and part of the dirt with a dark flesh pencil and short hatch strokes.

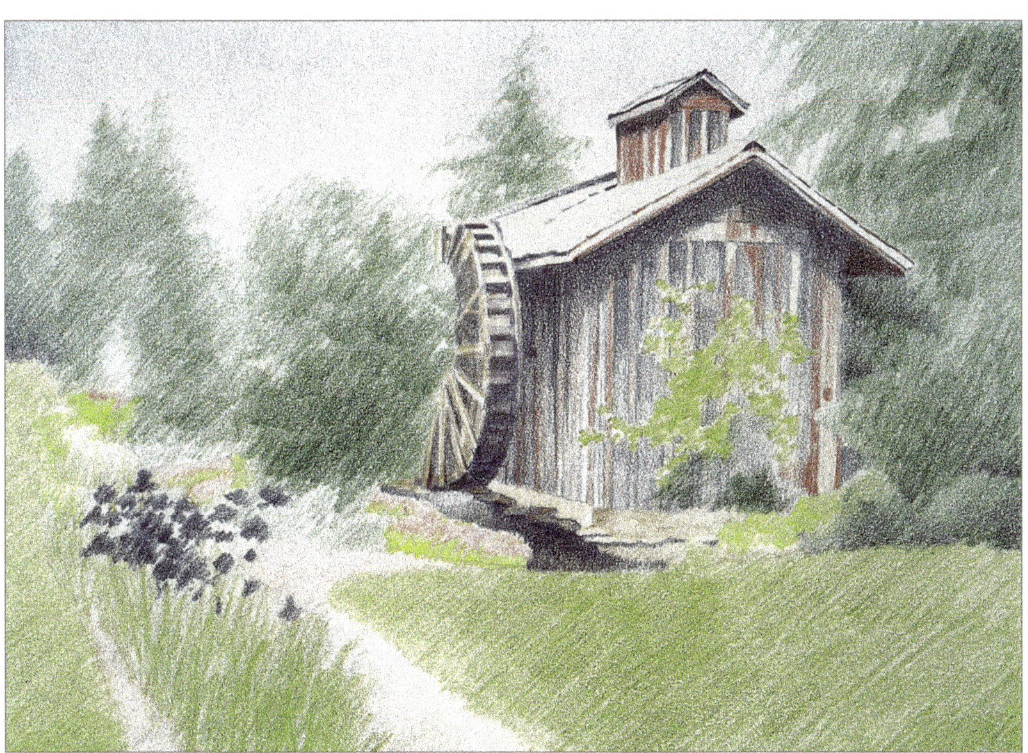

Step Three Next I use a sharp terra cotta pencil to make vertical strokes for the boards on the mill. I apply chartreuse to add warmth to the greens beside the flowers, under the pink flowers, and in a distant flower bed, using short hatch strokes. To create the dirt, I use a sharp raw umber pencil and vertical strokes. With vertical strokes of raw umber, I fill in the water; then I use the same color on the water wheel, making strokes that follow the direction of the wood grain. To create the dark gray wood in the building, I apply several layers of black grape with vertical strokes and medium pressure. Under the roof and in the water shadows, I use a sharp black grape pencil with calligraphic lines to increase the dark value. Then I apply celadon green to the front flower bed foliage, leaving spaces for a few flowers; I apply similar strokes with black grape to create the flowers. To add more warmth to the greens, I layer moss green on the tree against the building and in the flower beds.

Step Four Next I use reusable tack (see page 46) to create texture and dimension within the tree foliage, lifting out and reapplying various greens. For the dirt, flower foliage, and the yellows in the grass, I use a sharp ochre pencil with vertical strokes and medium pressure. Then I apply vertical strokes of pink madder lake with medium pressure for the pink flowers and over the purple flowers. In the flowers under the tree, I use the same pencil with small circular strokes. For the purple flowers and shadows in the flower bed, I use a dull dark green pencil with quick downward strokes and medium pressure.

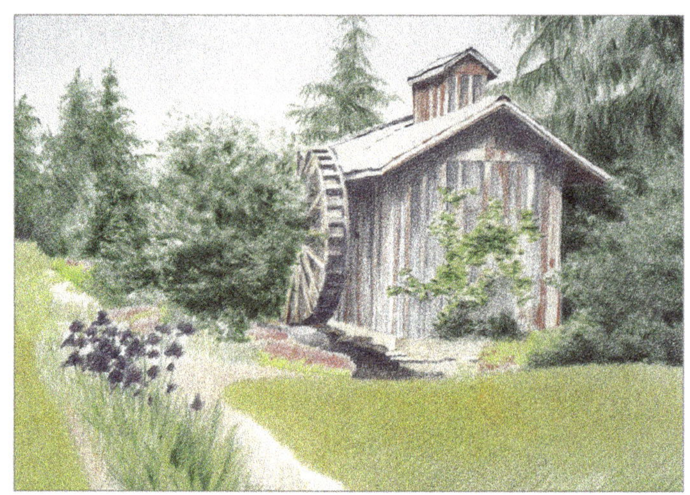

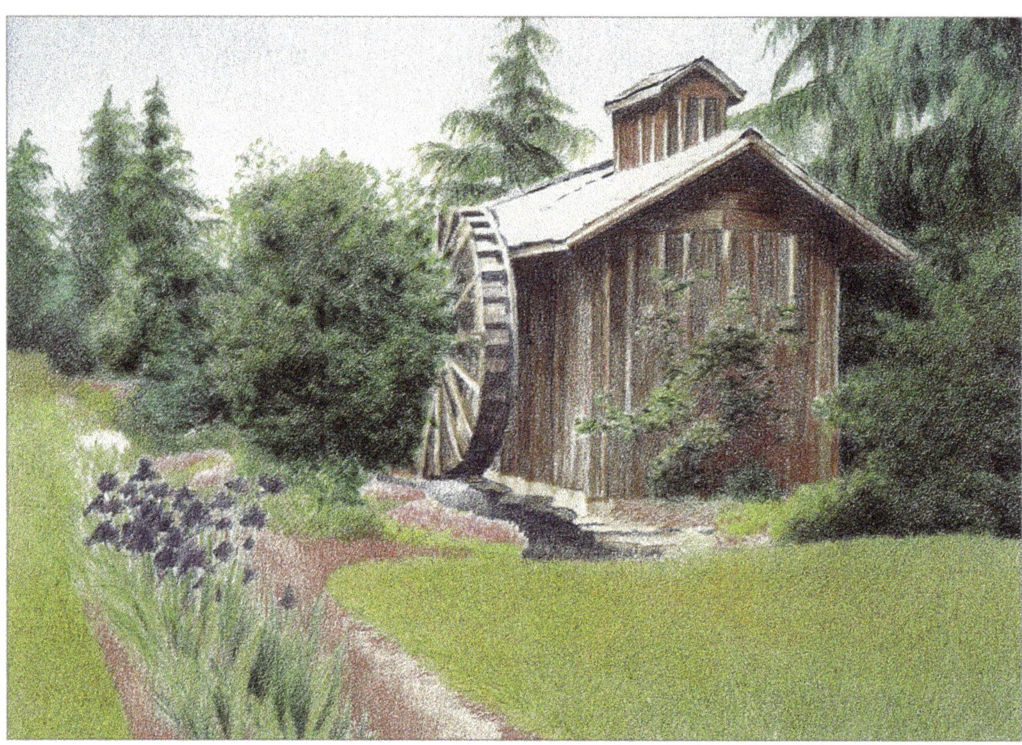

Step Five In the warm areas of the trees, I apply moss green. Where I want lighter areas, I lift out color with reusable tack, referring frequently to my photo and my value study to make sure I'm placing the values correctly. In the distant spruce trees, I use a sharp light green pencil with medium pressure and hatch strokes. I apply moss green to the grass with heavy pressure, using strokes that mimic the direction in which the grass grows. I layer terra cotta over the dirt with medium pressure and vertical strokes, leaving the lightest areas alone. In the building and the water wheel, I add dark values with raw umber, following the wood grain. For the rich darks in the trees, I apply a light glaze of Tuscan red, but I leave the highlights untouched.

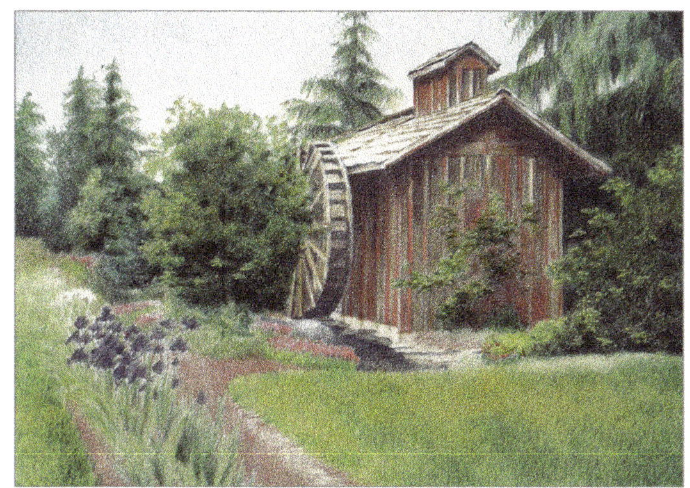

Step Six I add black grape in the trees and then create highlights by removing some pigment with an eraser. I use ochre and loose "X" strokes to create groups of leaves. To glaze the water wheel and the mill, I lightly apply ochre with crosshatch strokes. I add spots of moss green in the evergreens. Then I apply rose carmine on the barn and the pink flowers. For the roof, I use hatch strokes of raw umber to create the shingles. I lift out color to make a patch of dirt in the grass on the right, and then I apply a glaze of dark green underneath the tree in the same area.

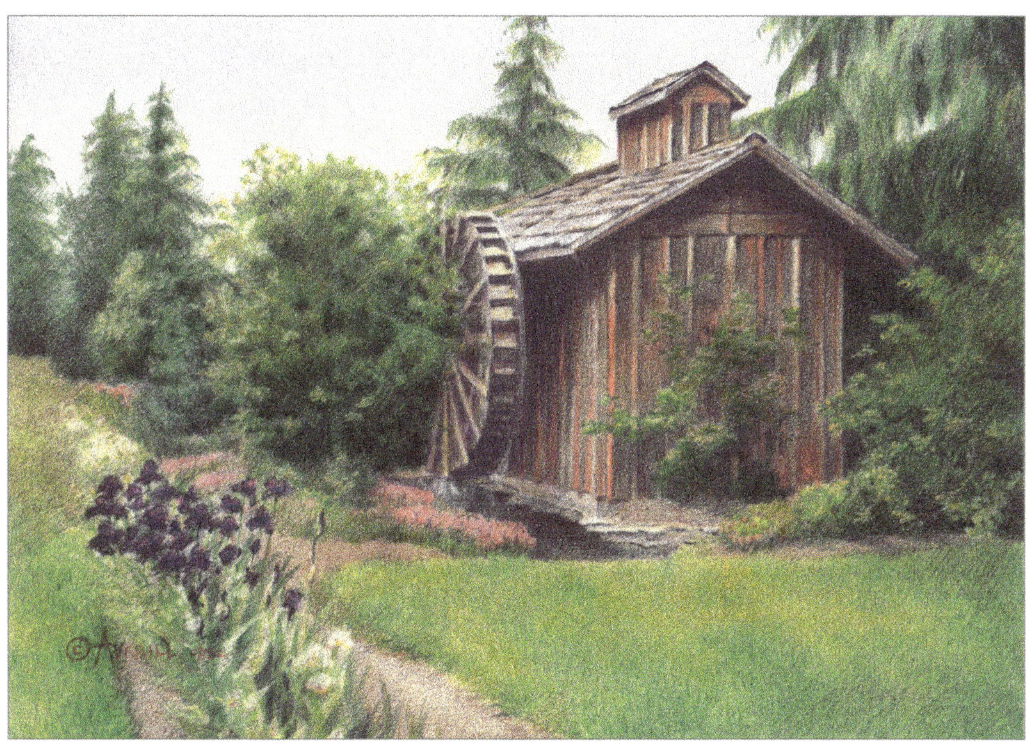

Step Seven With black grape, I create shadows on the water wheel and the building that follow the direction of the wood grain. In the front flower bed, I use a sharp black grape pencil to first outline and then darken the flowers; then I mix in rose carmine to add some dimension. I use ochre, dark green, and moss green in the flower foliage. To extend the grass near the dark flowers, I lift out color with tack and then fill in with moss green, ochre, and dark green. Next I layer dark green in the shadow under the large tree and the deep shadow next to the water wheel. To create subtle reflections of the trees in the water, I add dark green and black grape with vertical strokes and medium pressure. Finally, to unify the colors in the drawing, I lightly glaze Tuscan red over the middle and dark values in the trees, the flower beds, the roof, parts of the grass, and the dirt patch.

Setting Up a Still Life

with Sylvester Hickmon

Composing a still life takes a little thought and planning. Like a landscape, your still life should have a visual path that leads the viewer's eye in and around the drawing, as well as a distinct center of interest. However, with a still life, you are in control of choosing the placement of the objects and the lighting in the scene. When setting up a still life, try including objects of different shapes, sizes, and textures to help add interest and variation. And to avoid a static still life, choose an odd number of elements. Overlap the objects—don't align them on the same plane—and avoid horizontal lines because they lead the eye out of the picture altogether. In this beautiful still life, Sylvester Hickmon overlaps the pears and other elements and then frames them nicely with the checkered tray to direct the eye toward the focus of the scene.

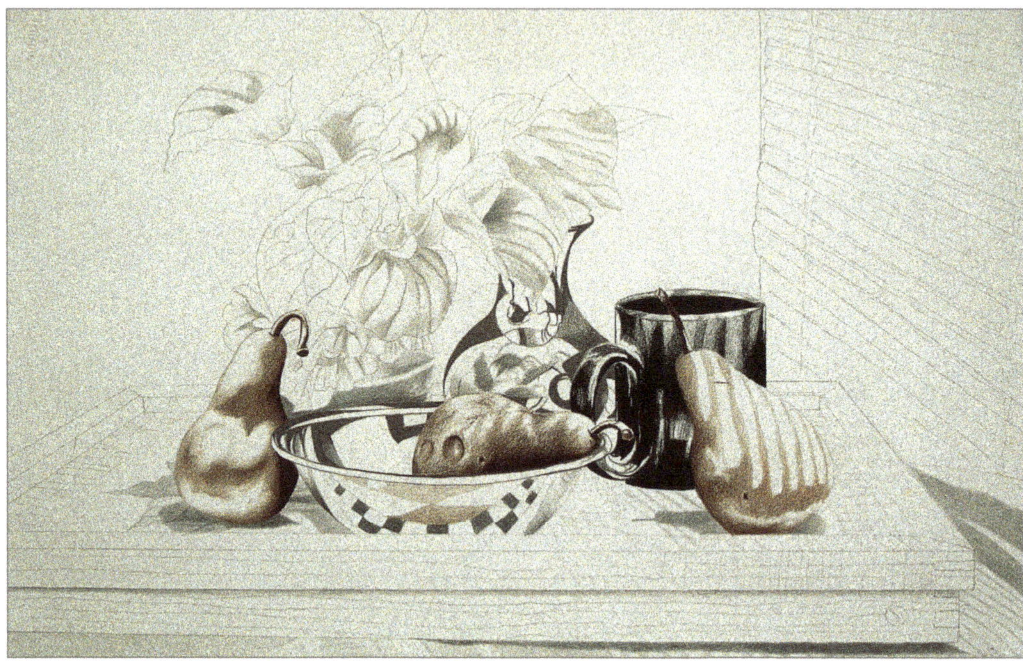

Step One As I'm composing this still life, I try several different setups, moving the objects around to find the most visually interesting arrangement. I also play with the lighting, photographing the scene at various times of day to find the most pleasing combination of highlights and shadows. Then, once I've settled on my composition and drawn the contours, I begin blocking in the darkest values of color. For the darkest areas of the pears, I heavily apply dark umber with a thick lead pencil, followed by dark brown for the lightest areas. Then I use a hard-lead dark brown to model the forms and soften the value transitions. I create the cup with thick-lead 90% gray and varying pressure. I add 70% cool gray and light gray for the reflections on the vase and then create the bowl with hard-lead 70% cool gray and light gray. I add dark brown for the reflection on the bowl and fill in the shadow patterns on the table with 20% gray. For the darkest areas inside the tray, I use 30% cool gray. I use a hard-lead light gray for the flowers but decide not to work on the leaves at this point.

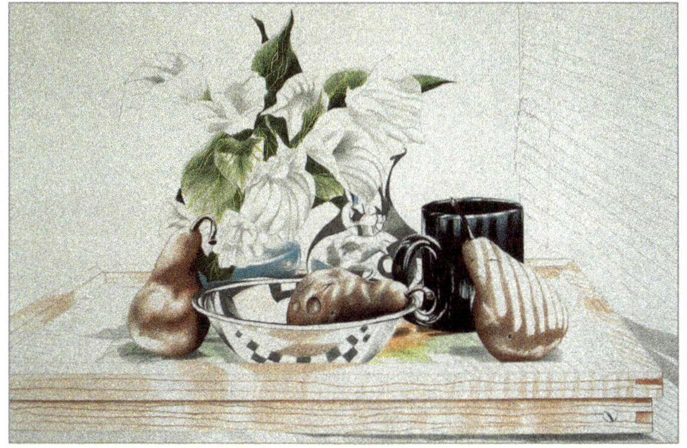

Step Two I layer indigo blue on the cup, burnt ochre on the pear, and terra cotta on the tray. Then I create the patterns and shadows on the inside of the tray with yellow-orange, terra cotta, grass green, and peacock green. For the inside of the bowl, I add light layers of cerulean blue and azure blue. I also use cerulean blue on the flower vase to suggest the reflections of the taller vase. Then I turn my attention to the leaves.

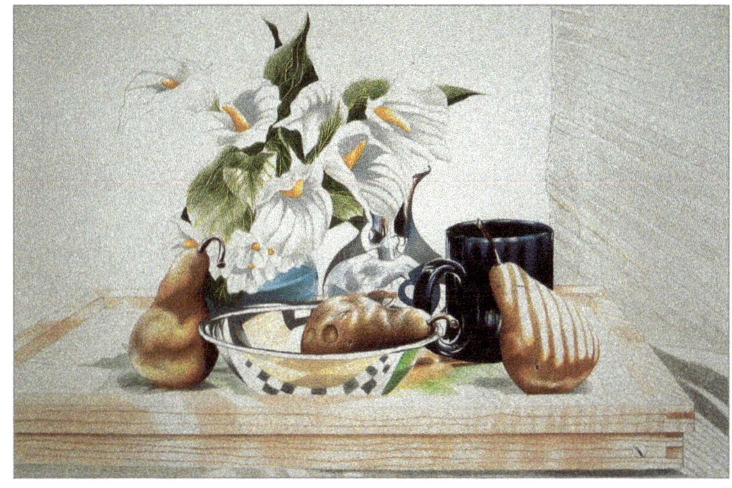

Step Three Next I use pumpkin orange and yellow orange to burnish the pears. For the pear on the left, I add additional layers of lime peel and yellow chartreuse. I use ultramarine blue on the cup and deco blue on the water in the vase. Then I add 90% gray, blue slate, peach, and 20% cool gray to the taller vase. For the insides of the flowers, I apply pumpkin orange and sienna brown and then burnish over those colors with canary yellow. I use 20% cool gray for the lightest areas of the petals, cream for the reflections on the tray, and apple green for the reflections on the bowl. Next I create the blinds with long horizontal strokes of 20% warm gray and add 50% French gray to the bottom section of the table.

Rendering Leaves

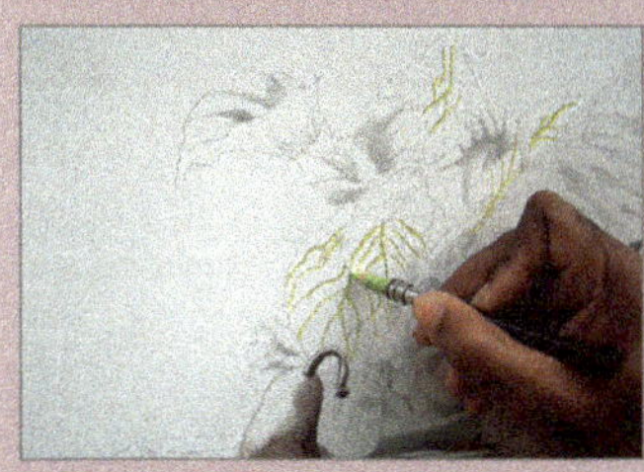

Step One To make the leaves appear more realistic, I focus on the details. First I apply chartreuse on the veins, filling them in completely.

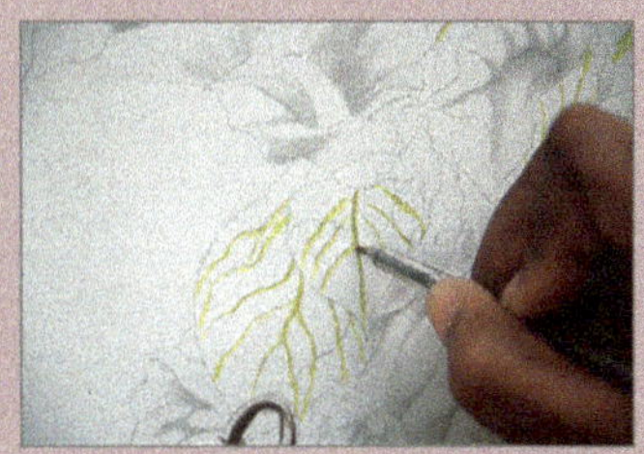

Step Two Next I go over the color with a stylus to impress the lines into the paper; then I reapply chartreuse to the impressed lines.

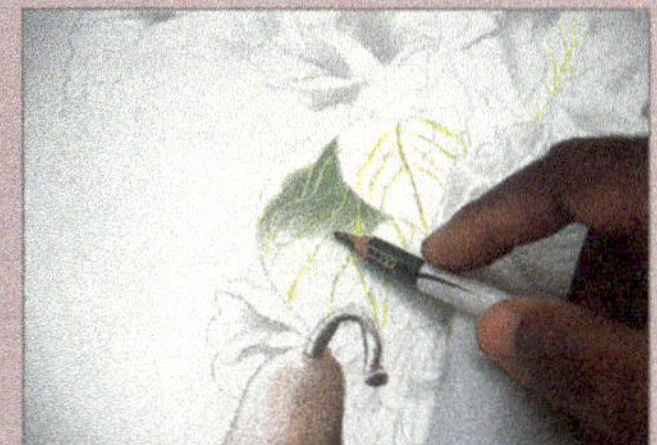

Step Three Finally I fill in the shapes with marine green and grass green, using the broad side of the pencil and softly blending the midtones.

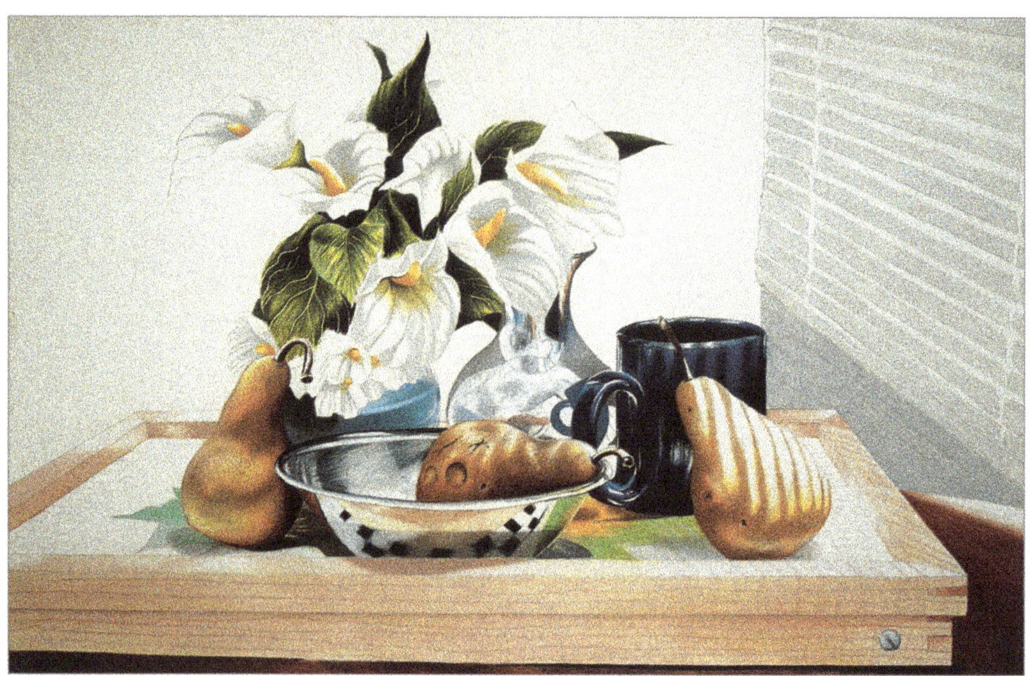

Step Four I use my stylus to impress pits on the pear on the left, and then I add layers of dark brown and mineral orange. Next I apply dark brown, canary yellow, and Spanish orange on the other pears and then burnish over these colors with a colorless blender. I darken the pattern on the bowl with 90% gray and enhance the shadow at the bottom of the bowl with 70% gray. I burnish white over the tall vase with heavy pressure and reapply the same blues and grays used in the previous steps. I use the colorless blending pencil on the cup and then add more ultramarine blue and white for highlights. I apply canary yellow to the flower petals and strengthen the darker areas of the leaves with 90% gray. Then I add more marine green and yellow chartreuse at the edges of the leaves. I apply terra cotta to the table and adjust the shadows with dark brown.

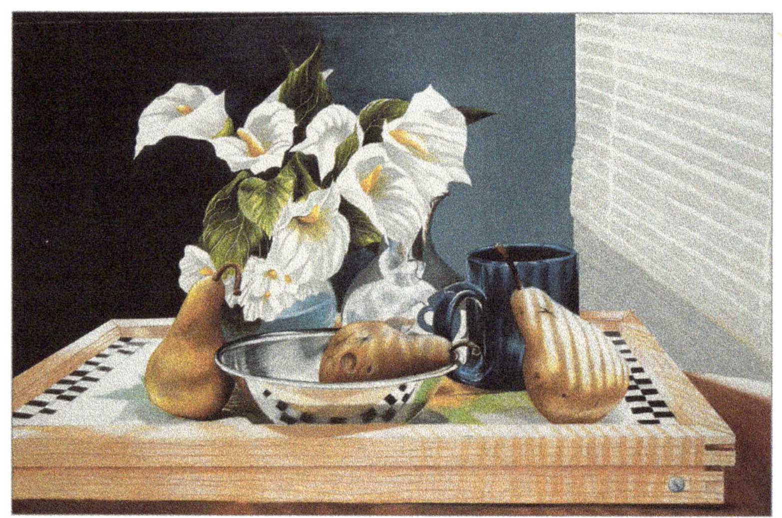

Step Five I fill in the left side of the background with 90% gray, then add indigo blue and blue slate. I use thick-lead blue slate to blend the colors and to create a solid backdrop. I use hard-lead yellow orange and hard-lead canary yellow to enhance the light on the pear. I apply white to the inside of the tray and use 90% gray to fill in the dark shadow patterns. Next I burnish the inside of the bowl with 10% gray. For the remaining areas, I use a colorless blending pencil and hard-lead white to clean up any rough edges and adjust the values as needed.

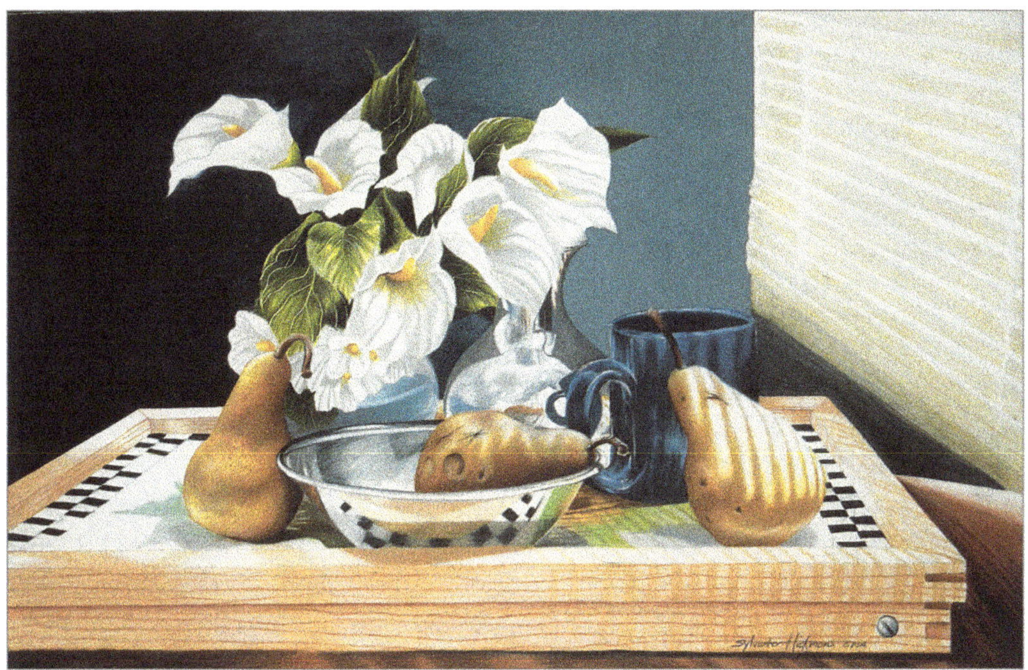

Step Six Now it's time to make some final color adjustments. I decide to add more indigo blue to the middle ground and adjust the bottom portion of the window blinds with 90% gray; then I add a layer of 20% warm gray to the top sections of the blinds for warmth. I darken the shadows on the tray with additional layers of mineral orange and terra cotta. I also use terra cotta to strengthen the darker lines in the wood on the tray, using strokes that follow the grain of the wood. Finally I use a soft paper towel to buff the image and give the drawing 4–5 coats of workable fixative. (See "Preserving Your Artwork" on page 63.)

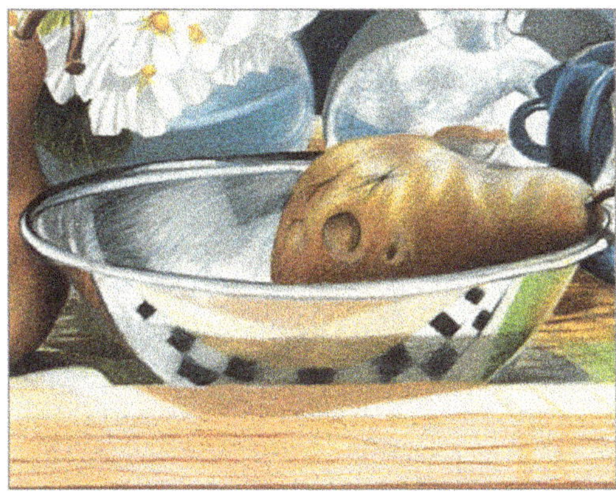

Bowl Detail I am careful to make sure the reflection of the checkered pattern on the bowl is not flat. The curved distortion of the image on the shiny bowl helps "ground" it on the tray and makes it seem more three-dimensional.

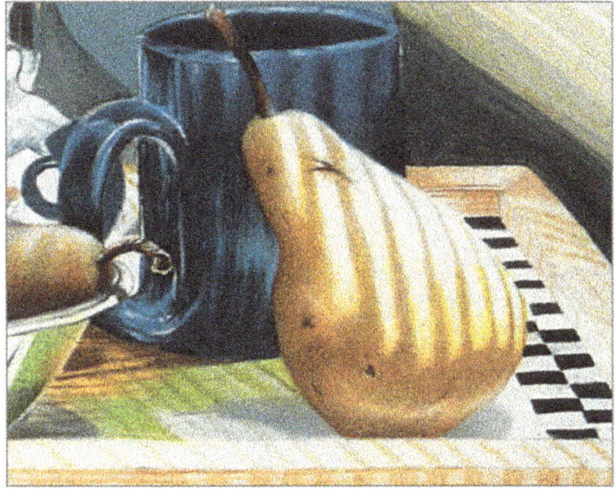

Pear and Cup Detail I use a stylus to impress the pits on the pears, creating a more rough and realistic texture. In contrast, I use a colorless blending pencil to smooth out the sleek ceramic surface of the cup behind the pear.

Creating Drama with Contrast with Sylvester Hickmon

The impression of light is what brings a drawing to life, and it can be soft and subtle or strong and intense. The eye is usually drawn to contrasts between light and dark because they're so visually interesting. And sometimes the contrast is so striking that the interaction or relationship between the two becomes the focus of (and not just a contributing element to) the drawing. For example, in this still life setup, Sylvester Hickmon manipulated the blinds to create an extreme pattern of shadows and highlights on the elements, making the subject almost subordinate to the play of light.

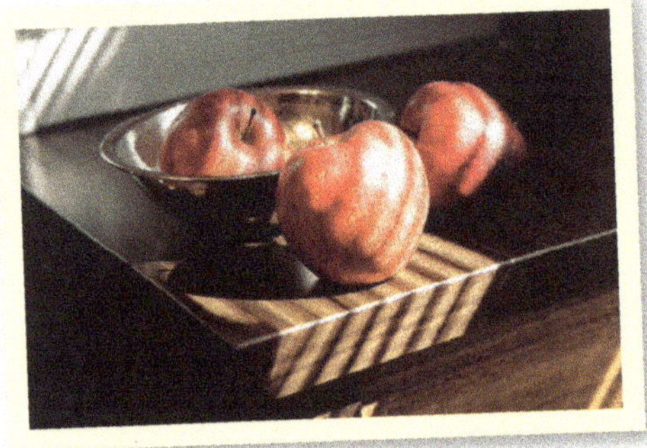

Lighting the Scene I photographed this setup from several different angles and at different times of day, experimenting with various lighting effects until I found the best contrast. I had to make sure that the apples weren't too washed out or too dark and that the viewpoint emphasized the angled pattern of the shadows.

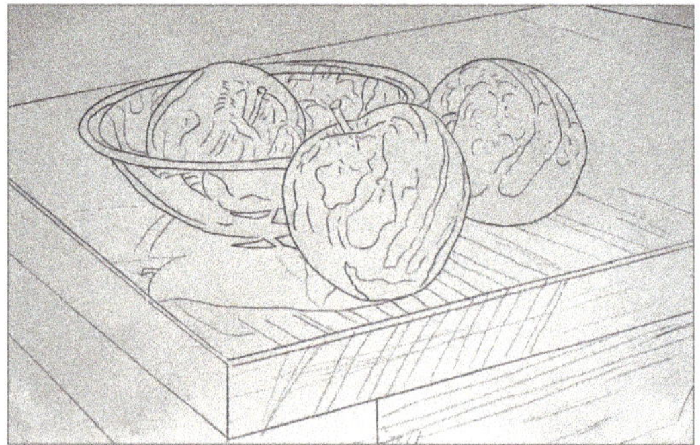

Step One I use a soft-lead graphite pencil to create a line drawing. I sketch lightly because light lines are easier to cover up, and I don't have to erase them. When I'm satisfied with the sketch, I use a stylus to impress the outlines of highlights on the apples.

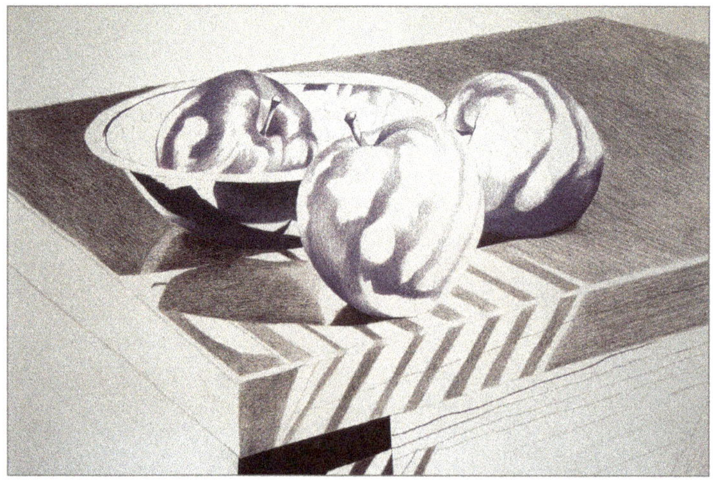

Step Two Now I begin laying in the darkest values and shadows to begin establishing the forms and creating the illusion of depth. I apply black grape for the dark areas of the apples, using the side of my pencil as I go over the impressed lines to avoid filling them in completely. Then I apply 90% gray to the bottom portion of the bowl and dark umber on the table. I don't color any of the background at this point; I focus my attention on the apples and the patterns of light and dark.

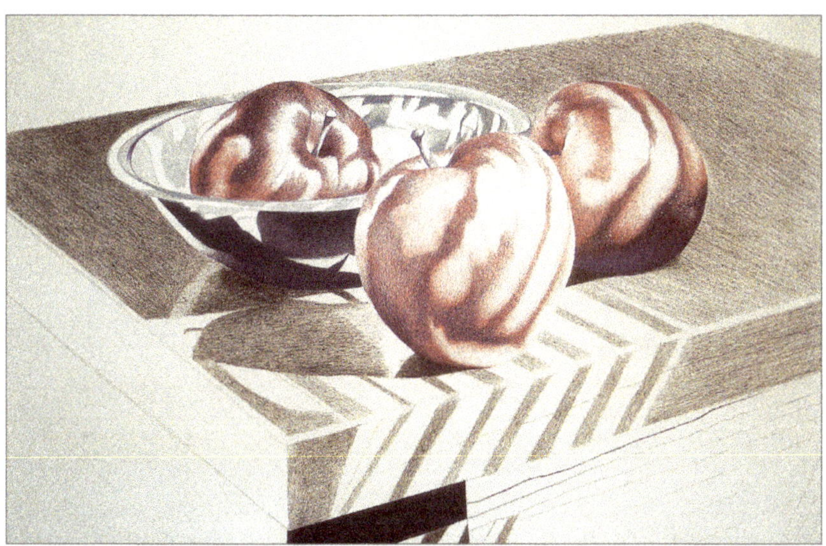

Step Three Once the darks are in place, I begin adding the midtones. First I use 70% gray and 20% gray to suggest the rim of the bowl. Next I use the side of a medium-lead Tuscan red pencil for the apples, applying more pressure for the darker areas and less for the lighter sections. Then I switch to harder-lead Tuscan red to apply more color to the apples; I often use both the medium and hard versions of the same pencils interchangeably to create softer transitions of values.

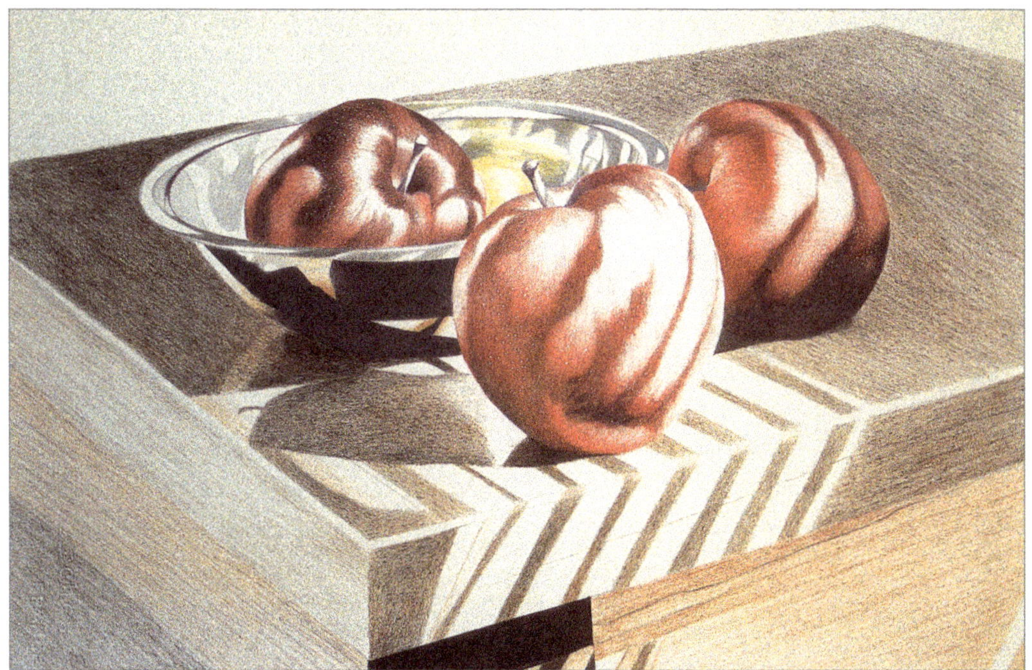

Step Four I use a utility knife to keep my pencils to a semi-sharp point, which helps control the amount of pigment I use as I build thick, opaque areas of color. Using both the point and side of a medium-lead crimson red pencil, I burnish the apples. Then I add 50% French gray to the inside of the bowl and burnish terra cotta brown on the top and lower sections of the table. I also add dark umber to the lower left-hand corner of the composition.

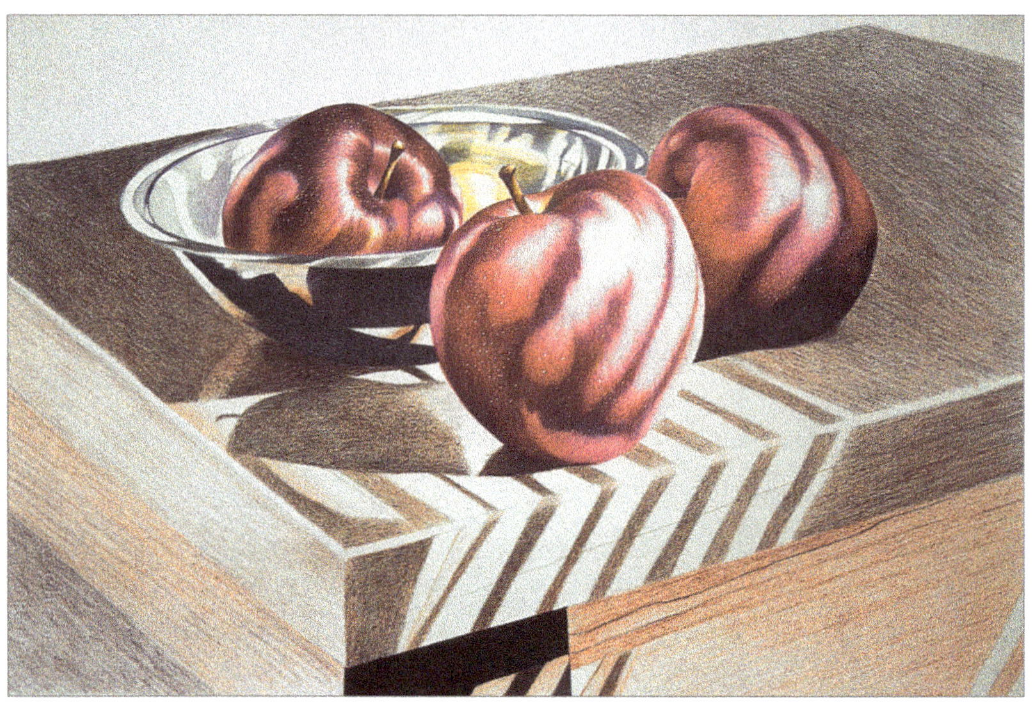

Step Five I use scarlet lake on the darker areas of the apples, and then I apply lavender and pink to the lightest areas to suggest strips of light. I use a colorless blending pencil to blend these colors together and to eliminate some of the impressed lines I created earlier. I also fill in the impressions by applying heavy pressure with the point of my pencil. For the stems of the apples, I use dark brown, peach, and lime peel. Then I highlight the inside of the bowl with 10% gray, goldenrod, and canary yellow. Finally I apply terra cotta to the bottom portion of the bowl to pick up the reflections from the table.

Using a Blender Instead of using a colorless blending marker, I choose a colorless blending pencil to burnish and blend the colors on the apple, creating smooth transitions of values. The blending pencil is a better choice in this example because it creates a more waxy blend—a finish that is better suited to the shiny apples and metal bowl. I also use heavy pressure with the blending pencil; the friction will help meld the layers of color. (Note that here I'm using a protective "slip sheet" under my hand so I don't smudge my drawing.)

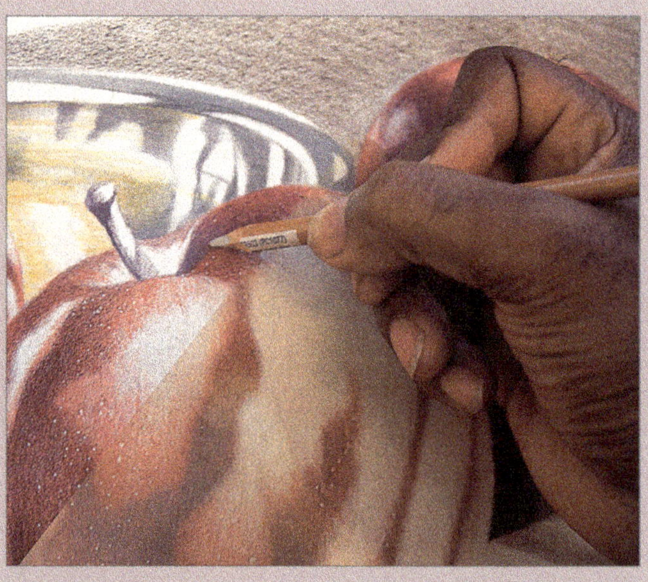

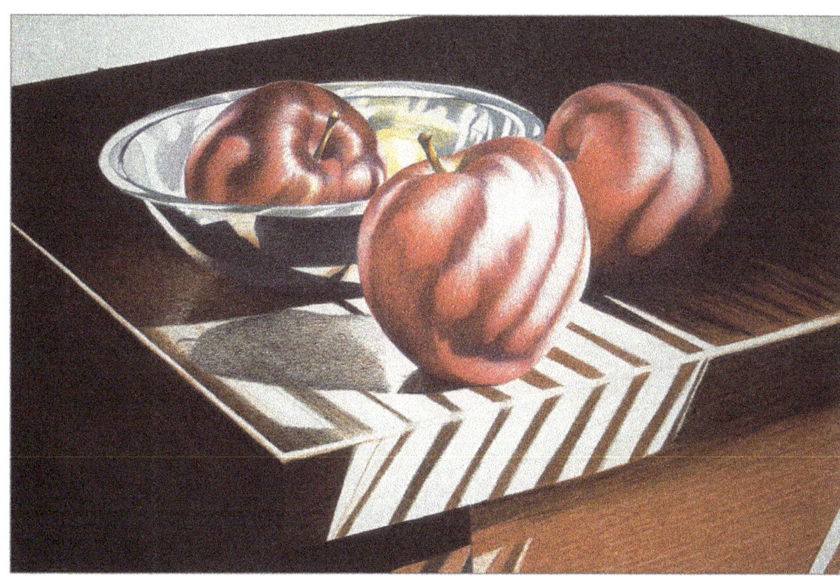

Step Six I burnish the inside of the bowl with white and reapply 10% gray over the yellow. I add indigo blue and deco blue to the outer edges of the bowl and add a few vermilion highlights to the apples. Then I extend the table nearly to the top of the paper so that the objects won't seem too close to the edge. Next I burnish the table with dark brown, terra cotta, and burnt ochre. Then I add dark umber and 90% gray at the lower left to balance the values.

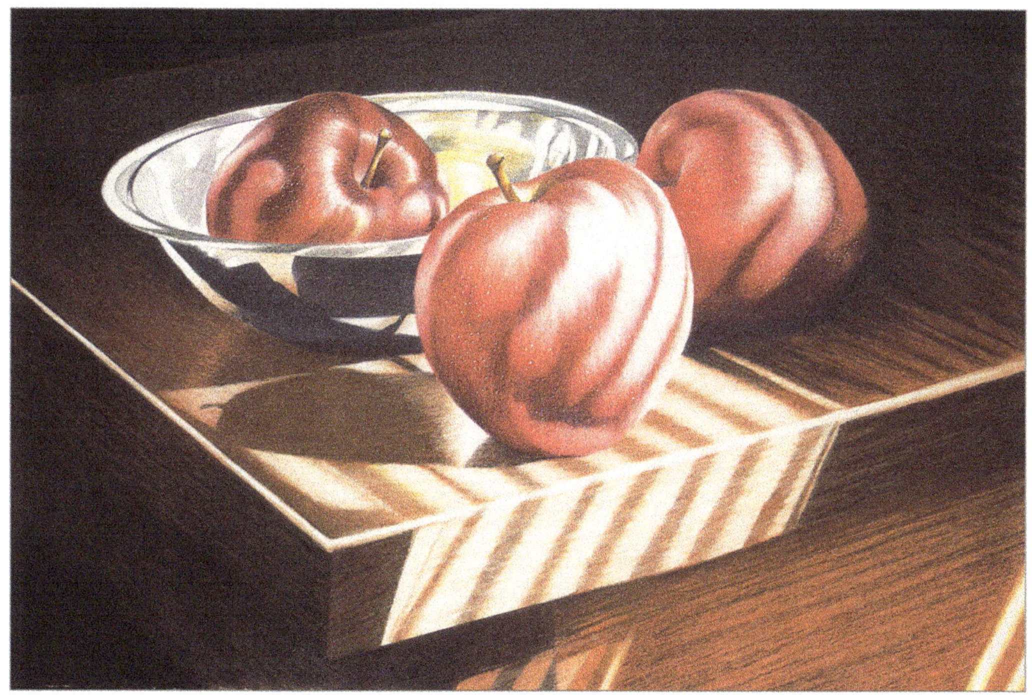

Step Seven I add canary yellow, Spanish orange, and sienna brown to the light areas of the table. Then I burnish over these colors with white and reapply the harder-lead versions of the same colors. I apply a layer of Spanish orange over the cast shadow of the apple (for added warmth) and then use a soft-lead black pencil to fill in the background areas. Once I'm satisfied with the final adjustments, I buff the image and spray it with workable fixative. (See "Preserving Your Artwork" on page 63.)

Utilizing Artistic License

with Sylvester Hickmon

One of the most rewarding things about being an artist is bringing your own personality into your drawings. You don't have to be a slave to your subject, replicating every color, shape, and detail. Sometimes you need to take liberties with your subject matter—especially if you want to add interest to a scene, improve the composition, or change the mood. When an artist alters a subject by changing the lighting, adding or removing an element of the scene, or enhancing the color scheme, it's called using *artistic license.* In this drawing, Sylvester Hickmon exercises artistic license to give new life to an old classic car by enlivening it with a new coat of paint and simplifying the background.

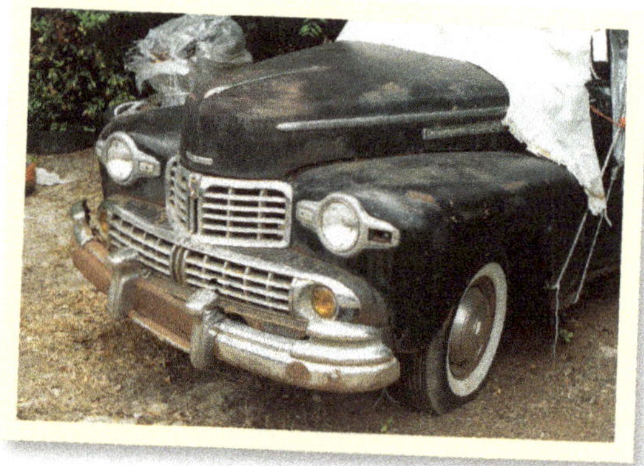

Breathing New Life Into a Subject I love to draw vintage cars and trucks. I often scout them out in old junkyards, garages, and backyards, searching for models that have just the right combination of charm and character. For this drawing, I chose a photo I had taken of a vintage sedan whose heyday is long gone. Now I have the fun job of restoring this rusted specimen to its original luster.

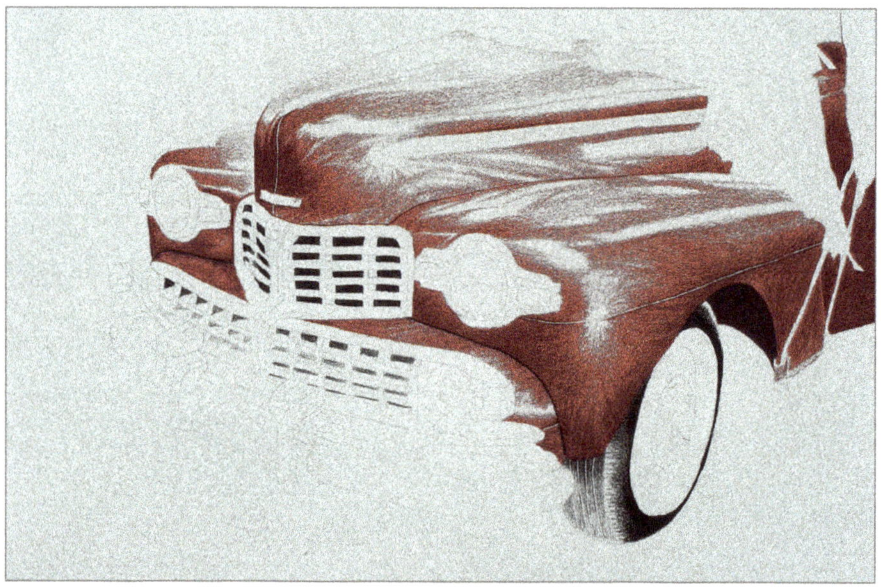

Step One I make a simple line drawing, editing the image to include just the outline of the overall composition and the darkest and lightest areas. I omit the trash can and any other distracting elements in the background. Then I use a soft-lead Tuscan red for the darkest values on the car, applying it with varying pressure. Next I use a thin, hard-lead version of Tuscan red to cover the same areas to ensure an even, solid application. Then I use 90% gray to block in the dark areas of the tire.

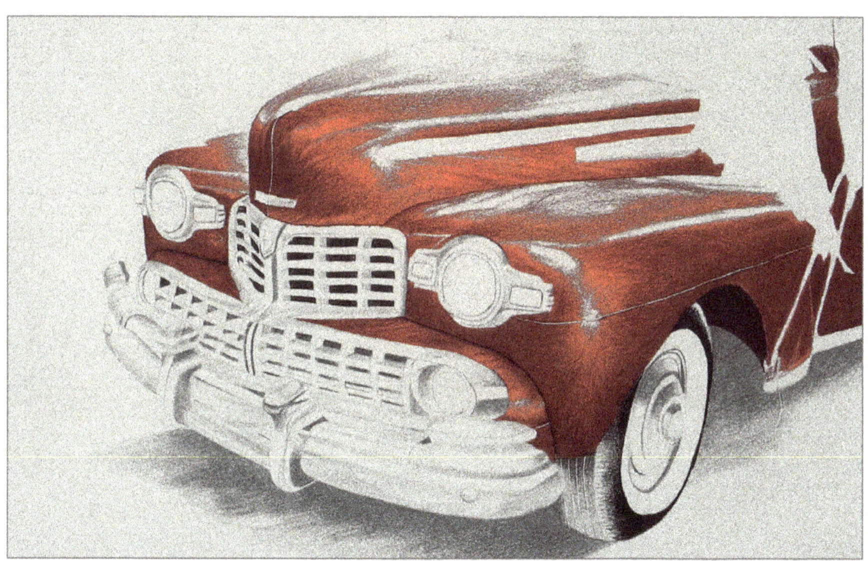

Step Two Next I use a stylus to impress the white detail lines I want to "save." I start to build my midtones with an application of thick-lead crimson red and medium pressure. Then I apply a light layer of white in the reflective areas of the car and add another layer of crimson red, followed by a layer of hard-lead crimson red. Since colored pencils are semi-opaque, sandwiching white between the layers of color can create a "glow" effect. Next I block in areas of the grill, bumper, and headlights with hard-lead 70% cool gray and use hard-lead dark gray for the shadow underneath the car.

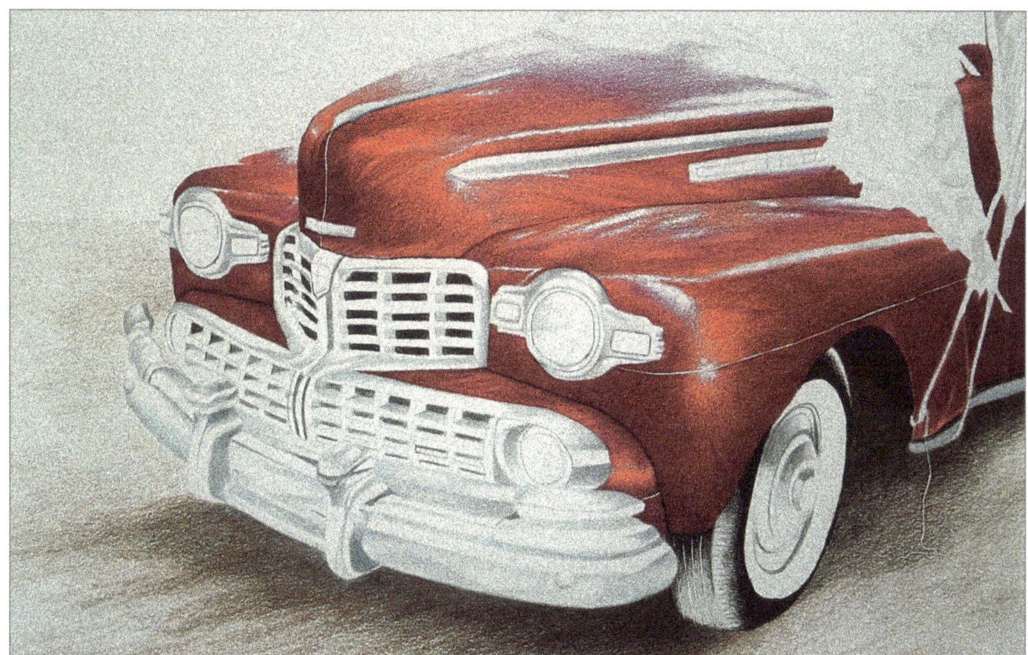

Step Three I begin building color by burnishing areas of the car using scarlet red and hard-lead rose with medium to heavy pressure. I use a thick-lead sky blue for the shadows on the grill, the bumper, the wheel cover, the headlights, and the hood ornament. Then I apply 90% gray to the tire. Next I start to work on the car cover with a medium to light application of 50% gray, and I add dark brown and terra cotta to the ground.

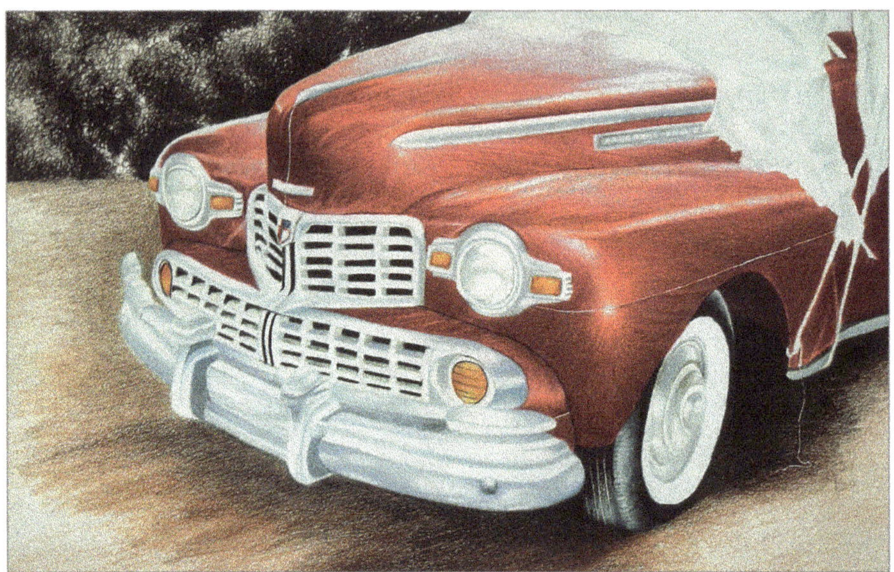

Step Four I continue to create the smooth texture of the chrome by burnishing it with 20% cool gray. I add details to the signal lights with terra cotta, followed by a layer of orange; then I burnish these colors with a heavy application of yellow orange. I burnish the car cover with white and then reapply 20% gray and 30% cool gray. Next I use white to add highlights to the lightest areas of the metal and to begin cleaning up any rough edges. I focus on the background next, applying black with varied pressure in short, circular patterns to suggest foliage. Then I fill in the ground with dark brown and terra cotta.

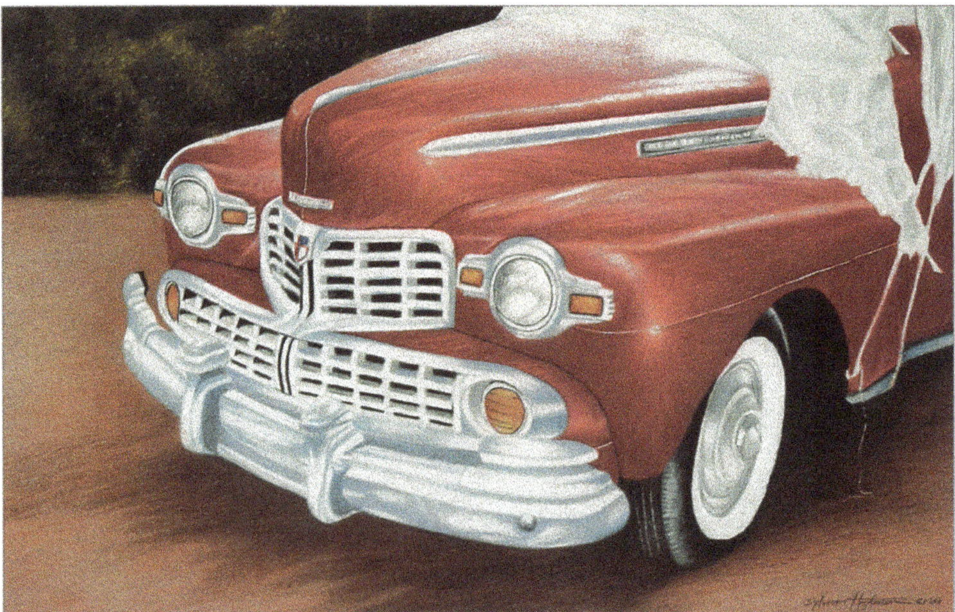

Step Five I continue to refine the image by layering, burnishing, and modifying color as needed. I use white and the colorless blender to clean up the edges and to fuse the values for a smooth, solid application of color. I adjust the wheel hub with 90% gray and then burnish it with Tuscan red. Then I complete the background foliage with marine green, yellow chartreuse, and yellow, and burnish the ground with medium-and hard-lead versions of terra cotta.

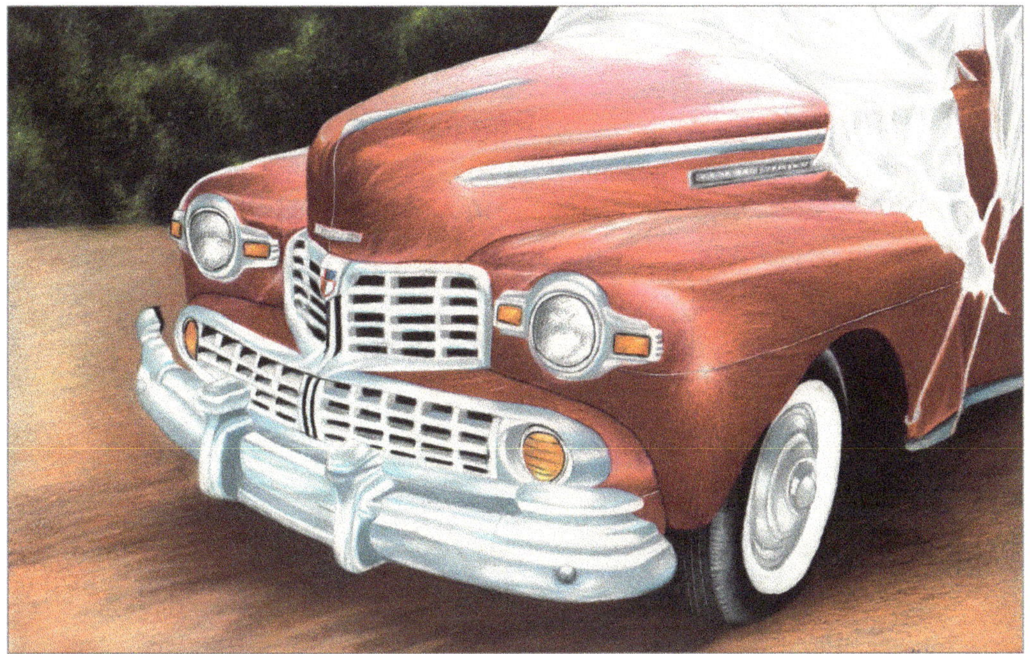

Step Six In the final stage, I continue to refine and clean up the edges with white and the colorless blender. I add hints of 10% gray and deco blue to the chrome and then burnish the areas with white. Notice that the lines I impressed in step two for the rope appear as the brightest highlights in the drawing. Finally I use a soft tissue to brush away pencil and eraser shavings and buff off the wax bloom before applying 5–6 coats of workable fixative to complete "Big Red."

Preserving Your Artwork

Once you've finished a drawing, use a soft cloth or paper towel to buff the image as shown below (left). This helps to remove the wax *bloom* (the whitish wax residue from produced by colored pencils) that has developed. Buff the lightest areas of the drawing first to avoid pulling any darker colors into them. Once the drawing has a polished, even sheen, apply 4–5 coats of workable fixative spray, allowing each coat to dry thoroughly before applying the next (below right). Spraying your artwork with fixative will seal the surface of the drawing and prevent the wax bloom from returning.

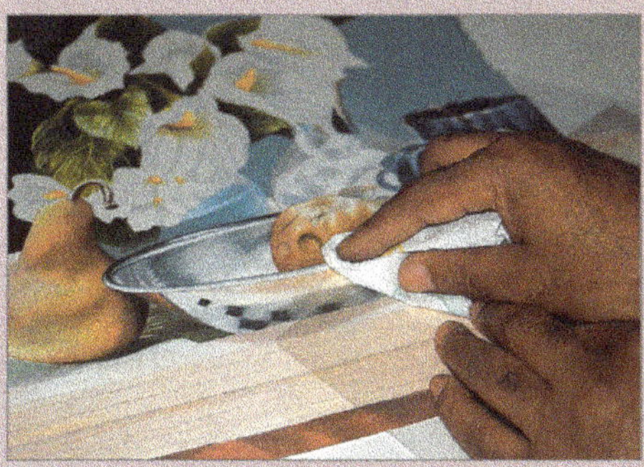

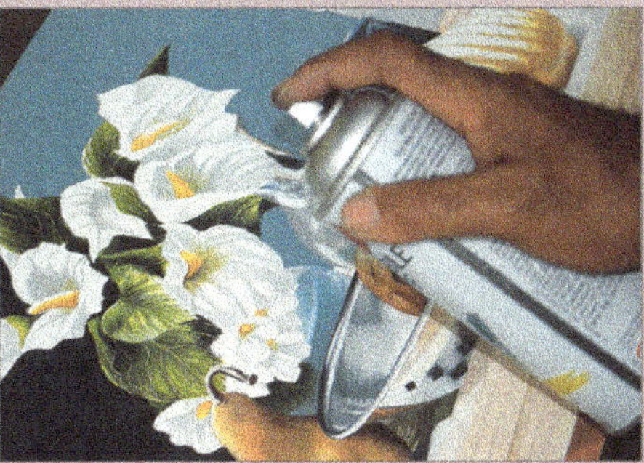

Conclusion

Once you've explored the variety of subjects and techniques these three artists offer, we hope this book will become a handy reference tool as you advance as an artist. Classes and workshops in colored pencil drawing are offered through many art centers and retail stores, and you can always learn more just from experimenting with other tools, techniques, and colors. Explore what works best for you, and keep looking for unique and interesting subjects to inspire you. Don't be afraid to try something new and challenging, and don't worry about making mistakes. Use your imagination, and soon you'll discover your own style and approach. Most of all, we hope you enjoy all your artistic adventures in colored pencil!

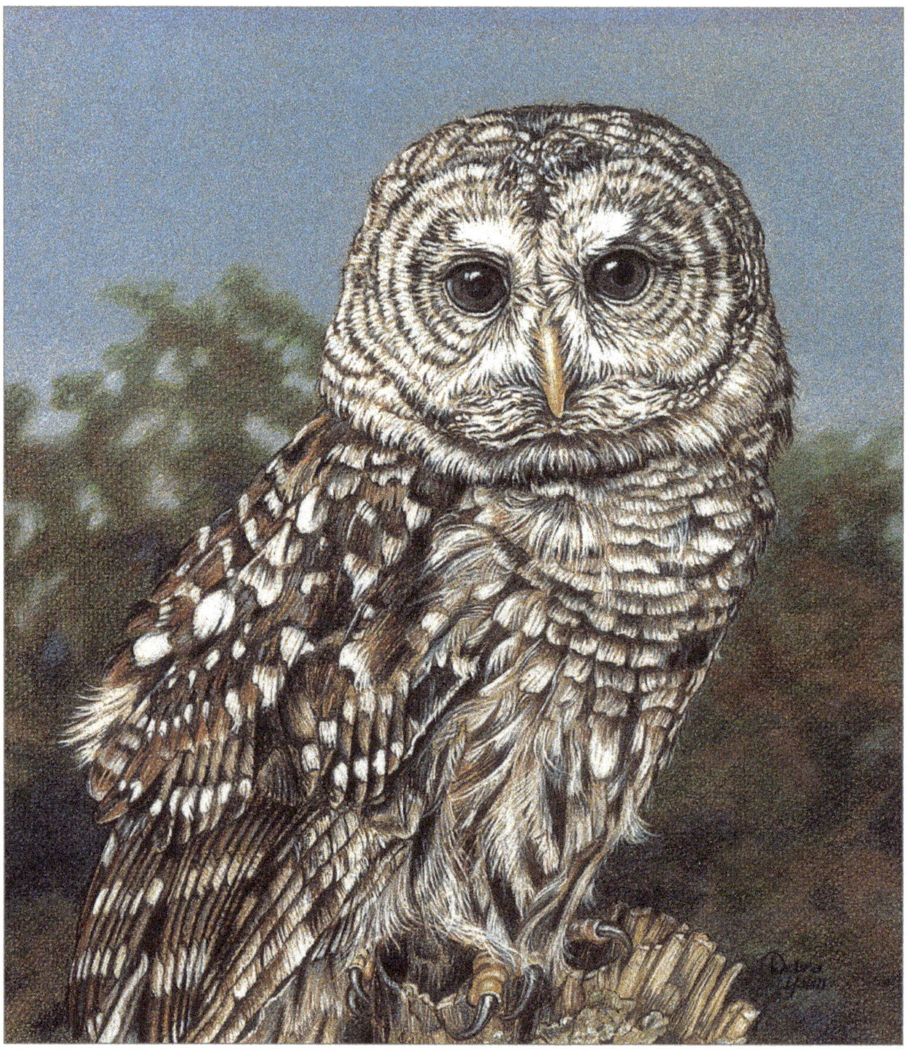

Jack by Debra K. Yaun

www.ingramcontent.com/pod-product-compliance
Lightning Source LLC
LaVergne TN
LVHW060758260526
839636LV00006B/10